DO YOU WANT TO BE WELL?

Do You Want to Be Well?

A Memoir of Spiritual Healing

CHRISTINE CHRISTMAN

Disclaimer: This book is memoir, a book of memories, and memory
has its own story to tell. While all the stories in this book are
true, some events have been compressed, and some dialogue has
been re-created. Some names and identifying details have also
been changed to protect the privacy of the people involved.

First Edition

ISBN (Print) 978-0-578-79860-8
IBSN (eBook) 978-0-578-79861-5

Cover Design and Interior Layout by designforwriters.com

For Roy Christman
1957–2016

And for my children.
You taught me how to be human.

CONTENTS

PROLOGUE

"The hope is that we can be a bell which rings out absolutely clearly without a flaw in it. Perhaps flaws have been carefully placed in us; almost like the flaws in marble that give it its beauty."
—David Whyte in *The Poetry of Self-Compassion*

ON THE WINTRY MORNING OF MARCH 18, 2016, I found my husband, Roy, unconscious on our bathroom floor. The blow knocked the very breath out of me. Neither my efforts at CPR—coached over the phone by a 911 dispatcher—nor the attempts of the EMTs who worked on him in our bedroom would result in recovery from that sudden, fatal heart attack. Grief invaded my world, unbidden and unwelcome. The scaffold of physical and spiritual healing I'd created over the past twenty-five years didn't just crumble; it detonated. Desperation drove me beyond my old coping skills, found sadly wanting.

In the early months of grief, I awoke each day between 3:30 and 4:00 a.m. to a panic attack—heart pounding, legs twitching to get up and run. I experienced a tumult of symptoms, from fatigue and loss of appetite to depression and severe anxiety. I couldn't sort out what caused what. Grief, while an acceptable diagnosis to my insurance provider, didn't satisfy me. I didn't like the answers I received from a stream of well-meaning and highly skilled health practitioners.

In the midst of my spiritual chaos, the holistic physician I'd come to trust stopped taking my insurance. I was terrified. Her unconventional approach had provided the map for my journey through chronic fatigue and fibromyalgia. Where would I find someone who understood my complex issues? I searched the list of physicians in my insurer's guide and found a primary care physician recommended by a friend.

Well, this is probably the best I'll do in the Western medicine complex, I thought. Armed with a file of medical history and diagnostic tests, I met with him. By then, the anxiety had gotten so bad that my entire body trembled. Friends and family would take my shaking hands and say with empathy, "Are you okay?"

I'm sure, in my first appointment, the doctor felt desperation oozing from my pores. As we reviewed my bloodwork, I kept prodding, asking him about different tests or tools to diagnose the problem.

"You seem to be looking for something definite here," he said, looking at me over his glasses in his lovely country-doctor kind of way. "I don't think you're going to find it."

Disillusionment set in. And yet, his comment contributed, more than any medication, to my ability to be well. My symptoms, regardless of labels, weren't going to fit the diagnose-and-treat model of Western medicine. Maybe it was okay not to know. Maybe it was okay not to have a definitive diagnosis for my cluster of psychological, physical, and emotional symptoms, the cure for which I could chase for the rest of my life.

In a simple comment, he gave me permission to accept my inadequacy. I allowed myself to explore my driving need for perfection in my health, work, family—every aspect of my life. Perhaps, as David Whyte suggested in *The Poetry of*

Self-Compassion, my imperfections were not flaws to be corrected. Perhaps in my newly emerging grief, allowing myself to be flawed, vulnerable, disillusioned, accepted, forgiven, and loved could transform my quest for healing into a practice of well-being.

If you, too, have found your world turned upside down by unexpected trauma, I wish I could sit with you over a cup of coffee or glass of wine and share my experience of sustenance. But the written word will have to do. Here you'll find not only a story of healing from grief; you'll also see how grief opened me to a vast, profound healing from my former interpretations of Christianity, which had oppressed and wounded me. I hope my story is a reaching out toward your suffering, a holding of your trembling hand, a dim light coaxing you forward. Or, perhaps, simply another perspective to illuminate your own.

Many years before Roy died, my need for physical healing led me into a spiritual journey. His death brought me to a fork in the road. In the aftermath of this trauma, I was invited to re-evaluate and reconstruct both my worldview and my day-to-day habits and rituals. I could accept the invitation life presented me, or I could reject it and perpetuate patterns that no longer served me. If life has issued you a similar invitation, I welcome you into my story. It's a journey away from the grounding Christianity of my childhood and into the vast and unlimited horizon explored in feminine spirituality, myth, science, and literature.

My healing journey started with a creeping sense of disillusionment. I was a thirty-something, career-focused minister's wife and mother of two. I traveled for my job as a journalist and educator in conference marketing. I kept getting strep throat, which made sense with the combination of traveling and raising young children. I engaged in round after round of antibiotics to no effect. When I complained about this to a coworker, she told me about her doctor.

"She's a little fringy," she warned.

Fringy. In the early nineties, the medical world was just beginning to recognize these less-than-conventional MDs as alternative practitioners. On a clear autumn day, I drove to her office, housed in a tiny stucco building outside of town. I met a woman not much older than me with a long, dark ponytail and a white lab coat over her jeans.

"This has to stop," she mumbled to herself, shaking her head, as she reviewed my records. She used terms like gut flora, sub-clinical infections, and Chinese medicine, none of which I'd ever heard before.

Under her guidance, I embraced the hope of alternative medicine. After each diagnosis, I stopped on my way home from her office and purchased the recommended herbs and vitamins. I changed my diet and found peace in the new possibility of diagnosis and a cure. Grains and dairy no longer found a home in my kitchen. My daughter opened the fridge one day and asked, "Is there anything to drink in this house that's not made from a nut?" I learned about the Meyers' Cocktail, a form of intravenous vitamin therapy, and chronic conditions like candida.

I discovered yoga, which was barely emerging in my small community at that time. My doctor said she knew someone (sort of in the parlance of "I know a guy") who taught yoga in a studio above a restaurant. There was no signage; you just had to know. This was before yoga studios could be found in every strip mall. Lucky for me, the instructor was from India and had trained in Iyengar yoga. I bought a yoga mat, bolster, and a strap from her, all of which I still use. You didn't just walk into Barnes & Noble and purchase those things. And Amazon? Still decades away.

My yoga teacher became my first nutritional counselor—she introduced me to sprouted mung beans and slow-cooked rice pudding. She told me how anger affected the liver and gallbladder and suggested calming yoga poses. She walked behind us in class when we were in downward-facing dog pose and slapped our butts affectionately with a strong, "Lengthen the spine." I studied yoga like an eager novice, writing down poses in my notebook with stick figures and detailed descriptions.

A practicing Hindu, my yoga instructor unintentionally led me to my first encounter with spiritual dissonance. During a session with my therapist, I asked, "How could she be living in darkness? She's the most gentle, loving person I've ever met."

Perhaps you're encountering experiences that challenge beliefs embedded in your traditional spiritual worldview. If so, I also hope you'll find in my story an invitation to explore new ways of redefining your spirituality. Each person's spiritual story shines light on another's path. In my confusion during the unknown, I relied on the writings of those who have gone before me. They gave me insight, comfort, and courage. And so, with great gratitude, I contribute my story to the conversation.

Seeking a resolution for the spiritual dissonance raised by my yoga instructor's beliefs, I quietly tiptoed away from the teachings of the church where my husband Roy ministered. I secretly traded my favorite Christian authors C. S. Lewis, J. I. Packer, and Frederick Buechner for Joan Chittister, Thich Nhat Hanh, Pema Chödrön, Sue Monk Kidd, William James, and Gerald G. May.

I tried traditional Chinese medicine, which was taboo in my community. No one in my church actually called acupuncture "the devil's work"; I just felt it was implied. One day, I saw a book on my Chinese medicine doctor's shelf called *Cutting Through Spiritual Materialism*, by Chögyam Trungpa. Thinking it was about simplifying and leading a less consumer-oriented lifestyle, I asked her if I could borrow it.

"Sure," she responded. She looked confused.

The book launched me into an entirely new world of spirituality and whetted my appetite for more. I practiced Father Thomas Keating's contemplative prayer and attended retreats based on Hindu goddess mythology. Roy wasn't far behind me—after ten years in ministry, he left the church and started his own business in our community. Our children were heading into adolescence. We committed to regular therapy and explored a variety of spiritual experiences, from Native American ceremonies to group therapy to Al-Anon. When Roy bumped into church members from his past, they often asked where he was worshipping.

"We spend Sunday mornings with a small community," he would say.

Our new community was Al-Anon, and we gathered with others facing their wounds in a meeting room at our local hospital.

Thoughts, stories, and experiences written down over centuries and shared in real time became guiding beacons, intermittently lighting my path and helping me trust in my next steps.

Two years before Roy died, my twenty-three-year-old son Sam and I attended Burning Man, a now-famous gathering of artists, hippies, and counterculture visionaries set each year in a desert outside of Reno, Nevada. The geographic footprint of the camp arcs in a half circle opening out to a vast expanse of sand called the playa. Perhaps a half-mile out into the playa is a wooden structure called the temple. The beautiful holy structure, adorned over the week with expressions of spiritual experience, burns to the ground on the final night of the festival: a symbol of the transitory nature of life and suffering.

Tall lampposts border the path to the temple. On my first walk out, on a clear day, I mused to myself about the charming effect of these lampposts. Very Narnia, I thought, remembering C. S. Lewis's *The Lion, the Witch and the Wardrobe*. On my second venture out to the temple, a dust storm swirled around me and I realized that the charming lampposts actually had a purpose. My long gauze scarf reduced the sand I inhaled and shielded my eyes, but the thick dust clouded my view of the path ahead. I could only lean into the wind and take the next few steps until I saw another lamppost, confirming my place on the path. I made it to the temple, hair wrapped in a turban like a desert sheik, dress whipping in the wind, sand coating my chapped lips.

My healing experience felt like that walk in the desert. Shimmering halos of light guided me through the haze of a blinding storm. The nuggets of gold I encountered as I sifted through the rubble of my old beliefs served as the lampposts leading into a sacred new journey—one that opened up to me through grief. I want to encourage you as you imagine new ways of understanding your suffering and healing. I hope these stories inspire you to find new sources of sustenance. I hope you will know both comfort and courage.

THE CONNECTION

I REMEMBER TELLING MY SISTER, SHORTLY AFTER ROY DIED, how in so many ways he was the major attachment in my life. (Losing a loved one teaches you a great deal about attachment). Roy and I were attached in a codependent way, asking a great deal from each other that we should have done for ourselves. I suppose most people are codependent at some level.

She asked, "Well, what do you attach to now?"

I paused for a moment and said, "I suppose God."

But I didn't feel attached to the God of my religious roots. Overnight, the sturdy cruise ship I'd called my faith had turned into a shallow dinghy, untethered and unstable, tossing me about amid a sea of unknowns. Who was I without Roy? Who was this God I was supposed to attach to? What made me feel safe and secure? Where was true safety and security? Did it exist? I was paralyzed with doubt about beliefs I'd spent my entire adult life constructing and trusting. Reading the spiritual journeys of others echoed my own experience: it rarely went gently. They rarely went willingly. It. Was. Terrifying.

Knitting, something I'd done for years, was recommended to me as a potential comfort. But I avoided it. I simply couldn't wrap my mind around following any kind of instructions or pattern. One day while binge-watching *Gilmore Girls*, I noticed an old knitting project stored in a bowl near the television. Heather-gray socks. It wasn't something to be knitted; it was a completed project I'd bungled, waiting to be unraveled. As

Lorelai and Rory tossed pop-culture quips around in the background, I walked over and picked up the socks from the bowl. I returned to my chair and let them sit on my lap for a long time, rubbing the wool between my thumb and index finger while images on the screen flickered in and out of my awareness. I picked up the scissors from the knitting tray, which was still—amazingly—sitting on the end table next to my chair. I cut through the single knot holding the sock together. I slowly, intentionally unraveled the yarn. It came apart easily, and I rolled balls of heather-gray wool and set them back into the bowl. Then I looked for something else to unravel.

Before I could begin piecing together my new self, I could only find comfort in unraveling what I'd previously created. Roy died in March. I unraveled socks and sweaters until October. Then one day, I started to knit. I knit twelve pairs of socks as Christmas gifts.

The unraveling and knitting together of my spiritual life took quite a bit longer. For the title of this book, I chose a classic Christian story of a sick man waiting by a mystical pool for the waters to stir so he could be dipped in and cured. Jesus approached the man and asked him if he wanted to be well. The question may seem either absurd or rhetorical to some, but I didn't think it was. Jesus asked the man if he wanted to do the work necessary for deep spiritual healing. To take up his mat and walk. I saw an archetype for healing there.

The healing miracle appeared to occur instantly for the sick man, but for me, a whole lot of unraveling and re-creating happened between "Do you want to be well?" and "Take up your mat and walk."

Suffering took me inward to gently touch, cleanse, and comfort wounds both old and new. I examined the possibilities of attachment to my divine source. In my desperation to find stable footing after the rug was yanked from beneath me, I returned to the spirituality of my roots. But I found myself, instead, taking it all apart.

Returning to familiar stories of Jesus's encounters with people who couldn't be healed by the medicine of his time—the adulterous woman, the man born blind, the woman at the well—I questioned what I'd been taught about these encounters. A new understanding slowly emerged. Christ connected with society's misfits; people for whom the system didn't work. Kind of like me. He made radical healing connections with those people. Attachments.

In every case, when presented with suffering, his offering appeared incomprehensible. People walked away saying, "Who is this man?" I wondered the same thing. And I asked myself, if Jesus was God, and all powerful, why couldn't he just heal the whole world? Couldn't he just hold up his hand and say, "I heal all of Jerusalem" or "I heal all of Judea"? Couldn't he have healed them telepathically?

Yes, but he didn't. He healed people in his relationship with them. Through divine attachment. Something happened when people opened up to this man. He looked into their spirit with laser vision and saw exactly what needed attention. He cut through defenses to bring people a sense of either ease or discomfort, depending on which would lead to healing.

I felt this connection for the first time during a college Bible study session. As a member of a campus Christian ministry, I often met with small groups for these discussions. One evening, we sat around a large oak table in a family dining room. I tried to share how the Spirit alive in the words on the page in my new leather-bound Bible seemed to click with the spirit inside me. I felt a genuine connection. I got really excited, trying to describe the experience. Eyes glossed over. The room went quiet. The subject changed. My felt experience was shut down by those who I thought were there for connection and support.

But instead of shutting me down, this gentle awakening nudged me toward more connection. I pondered this aspect of God. What was this "the Kingdom of God is within you" business? Could it be an energy permeating all creation? Humanity, animals, earth, and the heavens? An energy in me and engulfing me at the same time? Was it holy energy? The Holy Spirit? Could the Holy Spirit comingle with my own through some mysterious alchemy?

A few years later, I encountered a similar connection, but within my community. In the early eighties, one year into our marriage, Roy had attended Fuller Theological Seminary, where he had earned a Master of Divinity degree and a master's in marriage and family counseling. I'd audited a class with him called "Signs and Wonders." The class introduced young, idealistic seminarians to the emerging Charismatic movement and its emphasis on the Holy Spirit.

We learned about Charismatic Christians who believed in the gifts of the Holy Spirit: healing, visions, prophecy, and speaking in tongues. For twelve weeks on dark winter evenings, we met in a conference room on campus and practiced these gifts in a group of one hundred or so students. Leaders encouraged us to express visions and prayers and seek healing. Compared to the traditional Protestant worship of my youth, it felt like a spiritual free-for-all. The group moved from silent prayer to random members speaking in tongues, calling to the Holy Spirit, and sharing prophecies.

On the last night of class, we had planned to leave early to catch a flight home for my grandmother's funeral; I'd received the news of her death the previous day. I was a rookie at grief, having only experienced the death of another grandparent. We knew it was coming, so the phone call wasn't shocking. I immediately went into administrative mode, planning our flight to Chicago, packing, and finishing an article for my job as a staff writer for a magazine.

As the session opened, the leader had looked over the crowd and said, "A person among us is suffering the loss of a beloved woman in her life." He said if she wanted prayer, she should raise her hand and let the group know who she was. Along with everyone else, I looked around, waiting for this person to raise her hand. And I waited. And waited. Oh, I realized, tears forming in my eyes. It's me. How weird is that?

A connection happened. My suffering was witnessed. I experienced a spirit of compassion and comfort—I considered it the Holy Spirit. It sliced through my defenses and into the emotion I hadn't yet allowed myself to encounter. I didn't feel uncomfortable or exposed.

I raised my hand. People, including Roy, got up and stood around me; they put their hands on my head, back, and shoulders. I had felt safe and cared for as my tears spilled over, my unfamiliar experience with grief emerging into my being.

When, thirty years later, I encountered the intense grief of losing Roy, I couldn't find a way to draw on those experiences stored in my heart. I found it challenging to manage even daily emotions, let alone the overwhelm of loss. Some days I called my therapist two or three times. The emotions overwhelmed me. I sat on a couch in my mother's living room repeating over and over again, "I just don't know what to do."

Fortunately, my therapist did know what to do. In one session when the emotions got intense, he asked me to visualize my higher self sitting next to me. Maybe because my defenses were stripped away, I did envision it: a lovely, kind, strong, wise woman sitting next to me.

"Now, can you imagine her holding your hand?" he asked.

"Yes." I sat there with my eyes closed and she took my hand.

"Now, just let her sit there with you. Do you feel any comfort from her?"

And I did! This was new: I was feeling an experience instead of just knowing it cognitively. This was how I learned about comfort. This was how I learned, slowly, to comfort myself when I was overwhelmed by emotion. The cynic in me would occasionally pop in and say, "It's just your imagination." And yes, it was a magical interchange between mind and emotion. But then it started to dawn on me. Maybe this was what imagination was for.

Five months after Roy died, I still barely functioned. I lived on a diet of fruit and yogurt and the generosity of friends and family. If nobody brought food or invited me to lunch or dinner, I just didn't eat. I lost twenty-five pounds in five months.

I woke up each morning and moved from my bedroom to the couch in the family room. I lay there and read books without digesting the story until a commitment forced me out of the house. I went for walks. Occasionally I swam at the club. People gently suggested that maybe I needed some help. I, in all seriousness, asked my therapist if there were occupational therapists who specialized in grief. Oh, dear.

My sister suggested looking on Care.com for a support person to go to the grocery store and help with meals, laundry, and other daily tasks that had been routine until now. Just look, she said, you don't have to do anything, just look. Just look. It took two days to find the courage to walk into my study and get on my computer. A few days later, I picked a person and called. She led with a strong sales pitch that I tuned out. Obviously an experienced pro, she overwhelmed me with her enthusiasm. I cut the call short and took a long bath, watching the water ripple around my quivering knees.

A few days later, I tried again. Up popped the face of a young graduate student. I especially liked her response in the "years of experience" box on her profile. She had entered zero. An honest one, I thought.

I discussed this idea with my daughter. My adult children had so much concern for me that they both wanted to interview anyone I considered inviting into my home. They sensed a fragility in me they'd never known before. I emailed the young woman from the site, and we agreed to meet at Starbucks.

The day arrived. I'll have to get dressed, I thought—my only thought. I selected a sweater I had knitted and a gauzy scarf. I didn't want to look the way I felt. I wanted to at least appear competent to this young woman. But I couldn't. I sipped on my signature americano with honey and cream and let my competent twenty-seven-year-old daughter, Katie, take over.

"What's your favorite show to binge-watch?" Katie asked, drawing on interviewing skills unknown to me.

Kendra, the interviewee smiled. "It's kind of embarrassing," she said. "But I've been watching *Gilmore Girls*."

Katie and I looked at each other and laughed. So had we.

"Where did you do your undergrad work?" Katie continued.

Kendra beamed. "The University of Minnesota."

I actually laughed, and said, "A gopher girl!"

Roy and I had met at a college graduation party at the University of Minnesota, his alma mater. On our second date, he had taken me to the Minnesota State Fair. The dairy barn and the 4-H building were the backdrop for the seeds of a young romance, which bloomed in the corridors of the university, along the Nicollet Mall, aside St. Anthony Falls and Lake Como. Orchestra Hall and Dinkytown nestled in my memory with the special glow only a new relationship can cast.

And into my grieving world waltzed this young woman, bringing with her some of the sweetest memories of my life with Roy. Not only that, but she had come to Fort Collins to get a master's degree in occupational therapy.

Kendra came into my life and nurtured me back to my functioning self. As the days grew shorter and September quickly turned to November, she showed up at my house three mornings a week and gently coaxed me into conversation. She made tea, we sat by the fire, she suggested meals. She had just the right balance of competence, cheerfulness, and compassion. She quickly made herself at home in my kitchen and cooked up big batches of turkey chili and black bean soup to store in containers in my freezer. On the fateful election day of November 2016, we sat on my couch and cried at the results (just another sign my world was coming to an end, I was sure).

By Christmas, she had me out of the house shopping for gifts. (Though I told her I might have to leave Hobby Lobby if I had a panic attack.)

By January, we were cleaning out closets and reorganizing my kitchen. By the first anniversary of Roy's death in March, she drove me to the Buddhist temple to honor his life and sat in the sun while I meditated. By April, we were working in the garden and refinishing furniture. By the time she graduated in May, I attended her graduation party and wished her well. She assured me I was going to be okay. And she was right; I'd gained a significant amount of confidence in my returning strength.

People from Minnesota suddenly began appearing everywhere in my life. My new financial advisor was from Minnesota and had graduated from the U of M. My new dentist was from Minnesota, also having graduated from the U of M. Katie and I would laugh about it. But I chose to believe that something spiritual was conspiring on my behalf. I could dismiss it as coincidence. I could doubt it. Or I could embrace it as a connection to infinite love and creative reason conspiring in my life. I could feel safety in the possibility of a divine connection and let it be the gentle nudge helping me to trust life again.

I saw an allegory for this new kind of healing in the story of the man by the pool. It superseded the cause and effect model of diagnosis and cure. I saw a mystical connection between spiritual healing and physical healing. I grew curious about the relationship between deep healing of the soul and restoration in the body. And I tentatively opened to a new connection: a deepening attachment to a love I longed for.

THE WORD

WHEN MY DAUGHTER KATIE WAS SEVEN OR EIGHT YEARS OLD, Roy and I decided to tell her the truth about Santa Claus. One evening when Katie and I were snuggled in my bed reading *Harriet the Spy*, I told her. I expected a smile and a knowing nod. I really thought she would, as I did as a child, have known all along. We would simply confirm the nature of this lovely little myth and conspire to keep the secret from her younger brother.

Instead, she sat up straight and turned to look at me, tears forming in her eyes. "You mean . . ." She tried to bring her thoughts into words. "You mean you and Dad just bought my American Girl dolls and put them under the tree?"

I felt the fool as I watched her struggle between innocence and knowing. Oops—too soon.

I remembered her experience later when, as a forty-something graduate student, I took a class on goddess mythologies. I discovered that the stories shaping my Judeo-Christian world-view were also found in ancient cultures long before Christ walked the earth and far from Bethlehem and Palestine. When I learned of mythologies that included a descent to the under-world, days in hell, and ascension to another world, I wrote in my journal that I felt as though I'd been told there was no Santa Claus.

After grad school, along with working on my health, I spent the next ten years sampling a smorgasbord of spiritual prac-tices, from Christian mysticism to Buddhist mindfulness, from

Hindu goddess mythologies to New Age spirituality. I read the Christian mystics, Hildegard of Bingen, Teresa of Ávila, Thomas Merton. I read mythologies of the goddesses Inanna, Ishtar, and Quan Yin alongside works by modern feminist theologians like Elaine Pagels, Karen Armstrong, and Joan Chittister. At one point, I decided I was a yogini, attending a few weeklong retreats, meditating in incense-filled rooms, and hanging on stories of the Hindu pantheon.

My first yogini retreat was held at an intimate conference facility nestled in a forest in Northern California. I arrived on a spring day, bursting with anticipation about this sacred experience. My first roommate had already arrived and settled in, and she greeted me with a twinkle in her youthful eyes. She wore an African dashiki, and her hair had been carefully bundled into a bright turban. We found our cordial way through introductions; our third roommate wouldn't arrive until the next day.

I slept in a queen bed with deep, down-filled pillows and a comforter, a cool breeze washing over me through the windows above my head. I peacefully strolled to the dining room and ate my breakfast in silence. My roommate and I had just returned to our room, already shifting into a state of bliss, when something clunked at the door. Then there was a scraping, like a key trying to make its way into a lock.

We looked at each other. As my roommate rose to answer the door, it flung open and a woman who could have played Marilyn Monroe in a movie stumbled in, dragging an enormous suitcase on wheels.

"Hey, bitches!" she exclaimed in a raspy smoker's voice. "Glad to be here."

We became fast friends. She was a bold and adventurous wanderer who had explored radical spiritual practices like ayahuasca in South America—she took her self-proclaimed sacred purpose as protector and guardian of the plant very seriously. She had recovered from horrific abuses and found her way into a life of healing and balance. She was a yoga instructor. And she smoked like a chimney.

We fell into a routine, taking nightly walks after sessions. We shared a drink and a cigarette or two at a bar a few hundred feet down the road. One time, through a puff of smoke, she squinted one eye at me and said, "You have no idea how many yoga instructors smoke."

I laughed.

"People like to keep it pretty quiet, but I don't see the point," she added. "I am what I am."

The members of the retreat called themselves goddesses, and, like young girls playing dress-up, adorned themselves in flowy, gauzy clothes, draped silk scarves, and brightly colored tunics. Every day I marveled as my new friend pulled from her suitcase yet another combination of leggings and a gorgeous, wrinkle-free linen tunic. Or a handknit shawl over an elegant black knit dress. She never left our room without the signature red lipstick that circled the tips of her American Spirit cigarettes (only the blue pack).

Not the stuff of sacred spirituality I had anticipated.

The retreat leader brought to this practice her professional experience as both an actress and a psychotherapist. As we entered the sacred circle—a literal circle of chairs set around an arrangement of flowers and a bowl of floating candles—our leader sat in lotus position on a sheepskin rug, eyes closed, emanating peace. And then, after the meditation, she brought a delightful sense of humor to her teaching.

Of all the things she taught us over the course of seven days, I most remember this comment (and I paraphrase): "All spirituality throughout history has been created by men for men. And for much of history, spiritual leaders practiced in remote, isolated locations like islands, caves, and monasteries. Here's what I want to know. Where are the spiritual leaders who join me in my kitchen when I'm hustling up some breakfast and trying to get my thirteen-year-old daughter with PMS out the door in the morning?"

My new friend and I looked at each other. She winked.

Like a sunrise on a foggy day, a murky realization emerged. The narrow, rigid, patriarchal spirituality I had called home was made up in the minds of men. What I'd accepted as truth was really just people's ideas—inspired perhaps, but still very human. And the vast majority of those ideas were formed, shaped, interpreted, and recorded by men, for men. If the mythology informing my spiritual life was a garment knitted together by the collective evangelical movement of my youth, this realization was the loose thread. My spiritual wandering continued the unraveling, so by the time Roy died, it was nearly complete.

The culmination of this growing spiritual crisis—my dark night of the soul—came riding in on grief. I stood on the edge, looking into an abyss where my former beliefs felt insignificant. Everything I trusted had been abducted and shipped to some outer universe.

Maybe a person enters the belly of the whale or has a crisis of faith because they think they can go it alone. I did. My fierce sense of independence had me living in a relatively isolated place. Still recovering from the fishbowl experience of being a pastor's wife, even ten years after we left the church, I rarely exposed my vulnerabilities or asked for help. Then I reached the precipice of experience and understanding as I knew it and realized (too late, I feared) that I'd rather not go it alone.

I floundered, looking for something outside of me to bring safety, comfort, and peace. I tumbled into this unknowing without a choice. I read every griever's story and biography I could find, searching for the map. I simply assumed there was a prescribed way to get through this grief-induced spiritual crisis and transition to the other side. As time passed and pages turned, I realized the map I dreamed of didn't exist.

During sleepless nights, questions danced on the fringe of my consciousness. What did I trust to give me the ground I needed to stand on? What was steadfast in my journey through doubt and despair, anxiety and depression, fear and failure? What would help me shift out of a veritable soup of negative emotions and allow my heart to trust in positive experience again? It had always been love. And I'd found love in the Bible. So, like the prodigal son, I returned.

About a year after Roy died, I went to my bookshelf and found my tattered, leather-bound New American Standard Bible, its edges worn smooth from use. I flipped through the pages and felt a warm comfort as I saw my old notes in the margins—my neat, college-aged cursive, which had morphed to a more adult scrawl over the years; the ink that had bled through the onion-skin pages. Opening to the book of John, I read, "In the beginning was the Word. And the Word was with God and the Word was God." I found a mythology at its most beautiful in that first sentence. Mystery poured from that six-word phrase.

Why "Word"? I wondered. It was a question I could sink my teeth into. I saw new possibilities hovering around the edges of my old beliefs. I walked a few steps to my favorite reading chair and sat down, taking a sip of my fast-cooling tea. Out the window of my study, the dormant raised garden beds were covered for winter.

I recalled the scanty bit of New Testament Greek I'd absorbed by osmosis from Roy. The Greek word used in this passage was "logos." The online Oxford English Dictionary produced the following definition of the word: "The principle of divine reason and creative order identified in the Gospel of

John with the second person of the Trinity incarnate in Jesus Christ."

On the legal pad by my computer, I wrote, "In the beginning was divine reason and creative order." I pondered a mysterious interplay between divine consciousness and the Spirit. Christianity's origin myth begins with an infinite nothing. A liminal space. Then, some intention begins to create matter out of this formless energy. An intention, perhaps, expressed as the Word. Logos. Divine reason and creative order.

From infinite nothing, an energy of divine reason and creative order brought about creation as we know it. Man named the mystery God. Unfortunately for me, the word "God" was imprinted with scary patriarchal characteristics. A grand old man up in the sky waiting to judge and put the hammer down. So instead, I began to use alternative and interchangeable words such as Love, the Divine, Divine Love, Divine Being, and Divine Consciousness, all to mean this same mysterious creator.

German mystic Meister Eckhart said, "There is no concept of God that can contain God." Ah, but we must use names. And so, we do our best.

Out of this state of divine reason and creative order came language: language by which Love brought matter into being and named it. As the origin myth goes, a unifying source moved over the surface of the waters and took form, creating, sustaining, and supporting all life. Humanity lives and breathes this oceanic, spiritual energy called Divine Consciousness.

In this cosmology, where the material world and spiritual consciousness meet, I found a constant and infinite interplay of possibilities. Scientists use the term "quantum theory" to explain the interaction of matter and energy on the atomic and subatomic levels. My conclusion was that an energy called

Divine Consciousness was in constant dialogue with matter. And I, as spirit and matter, was a participant.

When Roy and I met, we almost instantly found a spiritual connection. But it wasn't the stuff of shared Bible study and prayer I'd been taught. Instead, Roy became the devil's advocate to my rose-colored spirituality. As the son of a small-town preacher, he'd had a peek behind the curtain of organized religion, and he approached his own spirituality with a healthy measure of cynicism.

About eight years into Roy's work as a church minister, I began to speak up about how the patriarchal theology in our congregation made me angry and uncomfortable. I ranted and rolled my eyes. In a way, he was already there—he'd experienced firsthand the damaging effects of group ideologies.

I told him I felt threatened when the men in our congregation exercised assumed theological authority. One had claimed that we had financial trouble in the church "because we let women serve on the board." Others insisted that women could teach children, or play the piano, or lead the choir, but not teach adults. And women could never, under any circumstance, have authority over men.

Roy became my sounding board. He'd listen on the way home from church as I pointed out the sexism in a sermon, the collective silence of women in a Sunday school class. He coaxed out my disillusionment when I found it difficult to articulate. Rather than offer theological corrections, he asked questions. We discussed. While he may not have understood the depth of my longing, he respected it. Maybe my longing touched something inside him.

I yearned for a pure and absolute experience of love—deep and abiding, beyond human limitations. I imagined a magical, shimmering, pregnant space between the swirling vibration of atoms holding us all together. What I'd been raised on, instead, was morality-based, patriarchal religion.

I felt like I was whitewater rafting and a group of men were standing on the shore, shouting at me. "Check your oar angle," they'd say, or, "Left side! Left side of the boat!"

I didn't want instructions from these men, who had absolutely no view of the white water ahead of me. I wanted someone in the damn boat with me, holding my hand and whispering in my ear, "Okay, good. Now lean right and feel the flow of the water beneath you. See the rock on the right? Just breathe and ride this next wave."

Patriarchal Christianity offered me a deity standing on the shore. My new cosmology located the deity within me as I explored how I connected to my Divine Creator.

When I'd ridden the white water in the past, I suppressed my emotions and instinct and placed my trust in the guys on the shore. I forced my brain to listen to and execute instructions while ignoring my own experience. Until I couldn't do it anymore. Until I could no longer keep my emotions in check. Then, the fear and exhaustion induced by tumbling through craggy rocks, and managing the raft as it hurtled uncontrollably down a waterfall, overwhelmed my brain and took over.

By the time Roy died, I'd listened to the instructions to suppress emotion and let my brain guide me for too long. I could no longer think my way through my experience. My entire nervous system collapsed under the weight of repressed emotions.

Could I, instead, trust infinite love to lead me through those emotions? I invited infinite love into the raft and used my intuition and felt sense as a guide. I turned the old, recommended way of spirituality upside down. I allowed emotion to be primary in my awareness and then brought creative reason to my experience of it. I learned to become safe with and aware of my emotions. I experimented daily with how to use creative reason to both process emotions and express my experience. But I'm getting ahead of myself. First, I had to learn about dignity.

THE WEDDING

I SAT IN THE FRONT PEW and turned with all the guests to see my only daughter walking down the aisle on her father's arm. At twenty-five, she was in love for life. Once Roy took his seat next to me, I surrendered to the emotion. I covered my mouth, trying to breathe as tears filled my eyes. After their vows, I stood on the dais with Roy and my daughter's in-laws, blessing the couple's future life together. My heart pounded in my chest in a way I rarely experienced. I thought it would burst with joy, gratitude, blessedness, and pride.

Roy, on the other hand, sat next to me through the ceremony grounded and sober, calming my whirling dervish of emotion. At the reception he shared drinks and gratitude with our guests as I let loose, dancing out my joy with each loved one in turn. He kept an eye on me as I worked through the chicken dance and YMCA. He quietly looked on as I drank the Italian sodas from the coffee bar my daughter had insisted on, embellished with tequila from my son's flask. Roy calmly waited for me to collapse so he could take me home, wrap me up, and let me settle into the aftermath.

I imagined Jesus as a similar calming influence at the wedding at Cana, where he turned water into wine. I pictured him standing by, waiting to be the designated driver, a half-smile on his face as he watched the revelry. Infusing a peaceful dignity into the event.

Then his mother Mary, who was seated at the table, noticed the wine was running low. (It's always the mothers, isn't it, assuring that all is well and everyone is taken care of?) She knew what Jesus could do and had the audacity to ask for it.

In Jesus's response—"Woman, what does this have to do with me?"—I heard echoes of my son's "Geez, mom, what do you want me to do about it?"

I imagined Mary looking up from her chair and raising her eyebrows. She didn't have to say anything else. She turned to the servants and gave them instructions.

I didn't necessarily see a beatific Jesus there; I saw a young man backed into a corner by his mother and left with no choice but to fix the problem. I heard Mary say, Just fix it, dear. How would you feel if it was your wedding and we started to run out of wine?

As the mother of the bride, I would've felt a flush rising to my face and the beat of my heart picking up a bit if I had looked to the serving bar and seen my guests turned away with empty glasses. Fortunately for us, the in-laws provided wine in excess, sharing the bounty. But what if it had run out? It wouldn't have spoiled the day for me, but it would have left a little haze of humility; a small lessening of the joy I wanted to share with my guests. No one wants to be found wanting, right?

After Roy died, I confronted an emptiness far more painful and vulnerable than running out of wine. I ran out of everything. I was emptied. I had nothing. I woke each morning to the bare essence of my being, no embellishments. My struggling ego had exhausted all its solutions. It was humiliating.

When the tears and snot ran down my face, my tunic and leggings baggy from three days (and nights) of wear, and my hair obviously no longer cared for, I was not pretty to look at. My neediness was palpable. I felt bare and raw and stripped of all dignity. And perhaps the most difficult part, the part I only saw later, was that I'd also been stripped of my usual defenses.

Like the host at the wedding, I was found wanting.

At his mother's urging, Jesus chose to address the host's problem quietly. When the servants returned with six stone jars, Jesus requested they be filled with water. The servants took those jars of water to the head waiter. When he tasted them, he discovered they were filled with wine.

In a single healing moment, Jesus preserved the dignity of the wedding host. Public exposure could have dimmed the joy shared by the host and his guests. Someone, after all, had to point out the empty jars. But Jesus showed compassion for the potentially exposed man. He helped him, as he did frequently in the Gospel stories.

Many of the ego-centered preachers of today might have grabbed the mic at the reception and said something to the effect of, "Your host has run out of wine! How embarrassing, right? But not to worry. In just a few short minutes, by the grace of God, I will remedy the situation for you and the wine will flow again." Then they would take a bow as the crowd cheered.

Certainly, Christ operated differently. This story hints at who Jesus was as a healer. The exposure of my flaws and weaknesses pointed the way to healing, but in the wrong hands, it set me up for humiliation. Seeing Jesus preserve the dignity of the host, I felt safer to trust compassion and the restoration of my dignity in the process.

Dignity protected my vulnerability as a grieving widow. Dignity, defined as conduct indicative of self-respect, came into my life riding on the spirit of generosity extended by friends and family. Dignity came when my grief was seen, validated, and shared. I learned that funerals, celebrations of life, and end of life rituals, done correctly, ushered in dignity for all affected by the loss. People who loved me, the kids, and Roy stopped everything they were doing to attend to his passing and to our pain. One friend drove twenty-four hours straight to eulogize Roy at the funeral. Others drove through a blinding snowstorm, only to be stopped by a closed highway just five miles from where the service was held.

Dignity showed up in every bouquet of flowers delivered to my house, every sympathy card gently signed, stamped, and mailed, every memory shared. Dignity gave me the courage to turn my face toward the sorrow. Each surprise guest, each time someone extended themselves toward our heartbreak, nurtured my ability to respect my experience. To weep without humiliation. To stand on my shaking legs and take one more step forward. I learned to trust that if I stepped into the emotion, sat with it, wrote about it, talked about it, I wouldn't be exposed and shamed for my weakness (as a lifetime of messages had led me to anticipate), but rather protected and encouraged in my healing.

I so wanted to engage with a grief experience I could have power over, one I could control. I was, after all, the mother who would've watched over those wine jars. I would've coached the bartenders to lighten up the servings as I saw the wine running low, doing everything in my power to make it all come out right in the end. When reading grief memoirs, I always compared my timeline to the author's. I made mental notes: had she gone to the grocery store yet? Was he doing laundry yet? How long until she went back to work? How many years later did she write her story? Although I wanted to find dignity in my ability to control, I instead found it in my ability to receive.

As the weeks of grieving dragged on, I was still desperate for validation, from whom I wasn't sure. I only knew that being found wanting was humiliating. This was no gentle humbling or coming to terms with a mistake. This was the disorienting humility of powerlessness. As a wife, mother, and businesswoman I'd experienced enough success and competence in my life to take for granted my abilities to thrive in this world. I knew how, when found wanting in other situations, to shore up my defenses, make excuses, beg forgiveness if necessary, and generally avoid a humble place of inadequacy.

In the depths of grief when I didn't have the presence of mind nor the faith to pray for help, friends new and old prayed on my behalf. My pots were empty. But in this emptiness, when I wasn't singled out to bear a public shame for my lack, I could enter more deeply into it. Powerlessness and humility didn't have to abandon me to a psychological and spiritual wilderness—they could, instead, be catalysts to healing. They could initiate the alchemical spiritual process, ushered in and sustained with dignity. This complex process included my struggle with depression, anxiety, and deep pits of despair.

A year after Roy died, I started working at a preschool, teaching one-year-olds. I noticed a philosophy among some teachers who resisted picking up children when they asked or cried. They didn't want to "spoil" the child by getting them used to being picked up whenever they wanted. I was mortified. In terms of a, say, eighty-year lifespan, a one-year-old is barely out of the womb. Building attachments (through physical and emotional connection) is their modus operandi. Yes, it was indeed possible to spoil a child, but not by picking them up when they cried!

I experienced the same attitude toward my grief. But instead of the concern about "spoiling," people tended to voice a concern that, should my sorrow be indulged, I would get lost in a dark hole of self-pity. Many grievers have a similar experience. Our culture is a good distance from the "snap out of it" mentality about grief, but it isn't beyond cheerleading. The bereaved often hear statements like "good for her, she's back to work" and "good for him, he's hosting the holiday party this year."

Seeing and validating me in my anguish and sharing support and comfort for an extended time did not push me further into the depths of despair. Those compassionate gestures gave me dignity: the dignity to be in my misery when I needed to, and to find my way out when I was ready.

Returning to the story of Jesus at the wedding, as the evening wound down, the head waiter tasted the wine and suggested to the host that he'd brought out the best wine at the end of the event. This was a departure from the accepted practice of serving the best wine before guests over-imbibed and then bringing out the cheap stuff when quality was less likely to be noticed. There's the miracle. Jesus had turned nothing (water) into something better than the host had provided. When I brought my worst to the experience of healing, I was met not with humiliation, but with the dignity of encouragement.

Was it possible that, instead of showing me to be wanting, my emptied self could open a space for something better than I could've come up with? When the ego had exhausted all its solutions, when I was on my knees and couldn't find the internal sustenance to bring more, an alchemical spiritual process began. The trickle of water in my wounded spirit transformed into a life-giving energy, enhancing the experience of being and elevating the positive aspects of life: peace, joy, love.

The Old Testament practice of public shaming and exposure—still used today in many ways—not only threatened the ego but also raised defenses. Should there be a threat to expose my protective strategies, my mistakes, my lack, my dignity, I knew my own reaction would be to fortify those defenses.

But with Jesus, compassion was always present in the background, waiting for me to run out of my own resources so he could gently step in and help me strip away my defenses. He wanted to comfort fears, attend to wounds, and help me find my way back to a full cup of wine, to the joy of life. Sometimes we don't even know the wine is gone or that a loving consciousness is operating in the background, making everything okay, saving us from the shame and embarrassment of exposure as we deal with an error of judgment or a crippling blow.

The designated driver waiting for me as I spent myself in the very efforts of life, Jesus stepped in and took over when I came to my end. My very existence relied on this greater power, higher consciousness, and transcendent truth waiting to bring me back to my soul, to the essence of who I was created to be. Without it, my defenses would stay intact—I'd shore them up and continue living behind my fortification, missing all I was designed to receive.

THE NIGHT VISITOR

I NEVER EXPECTED GRIEVING to be so much like giving birth. I've delivered two children, both experiences as different as the adults they grew into. Ten years into our marriage, my son came quickly, as second babies often do. At 8:30 a.m. I was chatting with my mom in the birthing suite, wearing the extra-large Chicago Blues T-shirt I insisted on in lieu of the awful hospital gown. The midwife came in, trying to be discreet about the crochet hook on the tray, which would break the membranes to begin the labor process. I had only a vague recollection of the labor pains from my daughter's birth three years earlier and (foolishly, in retrospect) felt the confidence of an accomplished mother.

My midwife's kind eyes and soft-spoken manner belied the tumult she was about to catalyze with a single sterile prick. Water gushed forth, and before the efficient nurses could whisk away the layer of water-soaked padding, the first labor pain ripped across my abdomen. The shock of it had me gasping, not panting, as my brain told me, Oh shit, I *do* remember this.

Roy went into coaching mode, watching the monitor and counting. I gripped my mom's hand, my control over my body ebbing away as the contractions moved through with alarming regularity. Roy counted down in my ear—six, five, four, three—as a contraction subsided. I caught my breath and asked to go to the bathroom. I figured I had about ninety seconds before the next contraction gathered strength.

On the way back to the bed, I doubled over and rolled onto the mattress. Contractions were supposed to come and go in a nice, rhythmic pattern, but what was happening to me had no rhythm and no pattern—it was just an unrelenting vice in my uterus. My body had taken over. The nurse checked. Ten centimeters. No surprise there. The urge to push overwhelmed me.

"Breathe, breathe. Don't push," the nurse said in controlled tones as her professional demeanor crumbled. She shouted down the hall for the midwife to return. *Stat.*

I could no more stop pushing than I could've gotten up and cooked breakfast. I had no choice but to surrender and let my body take over. The midwife came flying (okay, walking quickly) into the room, pulling on her latex gloves. She just managed to catch my son's head as he emerged. Then his shoulders, and then she coaxed me to sit up and gently take him under the arms and free him from my womb.

Birthing. A ferocity and then a gentle freedom.

Jesus used the metaphor of birth—one of life's most basic and visceral experiences—many times, but most powerfully in his encounter with Nicodemus, where he used the term "born again." Untangling this wording from the cliché I associated with altar calls and tent meetings, I revisited the story.

Nicodemus was a leader in a Palestinian religious sect known as the Pharisees. This collection of men considered themselves set apart as pious followers of the Jewish law written in their holy scripture, the Talmud. Jesus frequently pointed out their hypocrisy. As a spiritual leader, it would not do for Nicodemus to be seen talking with the nonconforming religious maverick. He had a reputation to uphold. And yet, he was curious. Curious enough to arrange a clandestine meeting. He wanted to know firsthand what this man was about.

Nicodemus must have thought the cover of darkness was necessary for his exploration of truth. I did. On restless nights when I struggled with fear, played out worst-case scenarios, or lamented a decision or choice, I opened myself to a desperate sort of curiosity that sought resolution, solace, and comfort. I entertained the possibility that something about my constructed beliefs had failed me. Nicodemus also had a suspicion about his religious education and rigid rituals.

The beliefs and resulting habits I'd created over time (and carefully preserved) were introduced to me by a therapist as something called "constructed-self": another way of thinking about the ego.

I thought ego was a bad thing. To have a very large ego, even worse. As a result, I'd put the idea of ego in a secret place where I hid everything I preferred not to face about myself. Like fear. And anger. And resentment. If I didn't see or feel it, it wasn't there.

But of course it was. Lurking under the cover of darkness. Because I saw ego as a bad thing and tried to pretend it wasn't running the show, it operated outside of my awareness. When I simply understood it as my constructed-self, and my true self as pure energy operating in the world in a human body, I understood my being differently.

In my early childhood, as my constructed-self took form in my body, mind, and nervous system, it responded to the world around it and learned what felt good and what didn't. I created a self who learned how to get my needs met.

Many aspects of my constructed-self were positive—my passion for reading, for example. Reading opened me to a world where I could process my life as it was mirrored to me in a quiet, uninterrupted space. Reading was a place of comfort and safety.

Other aspects weren't as helpful, like believing that taking care of others was more important than self-care. Like trying to control my environment and the people around me so I could be protected from my intense emotions. Like smiling a lot and listening to other people so I would be accepted into the community.

In the early months of grief, I spent a great deal of lonely time at home. My daughter called it our "staring at the walls" period. But I still met with my therapist regularly, gently examining the raw self who had nowhere to go and nothing to do. As I inevitably compared my previous life to my current void, I saw my constructed-self as an elaborate set of spinning plates I worked very hard to keep in the air.

In the year before Roy died, I was trying to start a new business of my own to sustain my professional self. I was helping at Roy's office a few days a week as the supportive wife. I was taking care of my mother in the wake of my father's death as the caring daughter. I was working on a new book, trying to nurture my creative self. I was making sixty-mile trips to visit my daughter as she began her new married life, ever the supportive mom. I had wine dates with friends and participated in book groups, nurturing long-held friendships. And on it went.

I believed that if even one plate wobbled, all of me would come tumbling down. I would be so ashamed when the world saw I wasn't the person I told everyone I was: the constructed-self, the fragile and fiercely protected self. And so I found myself, stopped cold in the throes of grief, struggling not with just a few wobbling plates, but with piles of broken stoneware at my feet.

Deceiving myself was, of course, the most challenging of deceptions. My magical plate-spinning may have convinced others, but when I sat down with myself—when I probed the places I would've rather kept in the dark—those deceptions didn't work as well.

Like Nicodemus, when my interior was illuminated, I had to believe (or be helped to believe) that I had the courage to see those constructed pieces of myself and make choices about what to keep and what to discard. This journey away from my familiar self felt like suffering. In the first stages of grief, when the emotion was so intense, so overwhelming, I knew—like in my birthing experience—I could do nothing but surrender to it. I fought and fought, but in the end, I didn't have a choice.

In the story, when confronted, Nicodemus pulled out the best of his constructed-self. He began, as all good politicians do, with flattery. He called Jesus "Rabbi" and said, "We know that you come from God as a teacher, for no one can do these signs that you do unless God is with him."

This comment made me want to ask, where are you going with this, Nic? But Jesus didn't waste time on inquiries. He got right to the point, saying, "Unless one is born again, he cannot see the kingdom of God."

There it was. Born again. Revisiting this story, I found it curious that Jesus began a conversation with an educated, intellectual man about a uniquely feminine experience.

I imagined Nicodemus becoming disoriented, as I did whenever I lost control of a conversation. (Especially one with Roy.) Jesus had gently led him out of his normal range of thought and experience into a sacred space. Or tried to.

But then Nicodemus brought out his next defense: intellectual processing. (One of my favorites, by the way.) He asked Jesus, "How can a man be born when he is old? He cannot enter a second time into his mother's womb and be born, can he?"

Jesus answered, "Unless one is born of water and the Spirit, he cannot enter into the kingdom of God. That which is born of the flesh is flesh, and that which is born of the Spirit is spirit. Do not marvel that I said to you, 'You must be born again.'"

Jesus described a different type of birth. Not a birth of flesh and bone, but a birth of water and spirit. This spiritual disrobing, this removing of the constructed-self, Jesus seemed to be saying, could lead to a different life. But Nicodemus, the teacher of Israel, didn't quite get what Jesus was telling him.

In my grieving, the possibility of a spiritual birth opened up to me on the wave of extreme emotion. Both birth (bringing into the world) and death (letting go of the world) required deep suffering, physically as well as spiritually. In the transformation born out of grief, my heart broke open and the self I'd constructed to protect me from emotion released.

I'd erected a Hoover Dam against my emotions, and the release was a gushing torrent I couldn't contain no matter how hard I fought. A psychologist once described it to me as a bottle of soda: as long as the lid stayed on, you could shake it quite a bit and keep the bubbles contained. But once the lid came off, the pent-up energy exploded. Trauma both shook the bottle (intensified the emotional experience) and popped the lid.

While in the early stages of processing her own grief, my daughter told a story about how unfamiliar I became in the first hours after Roy died. By the time I returned from the hospital, family had begun to gather in the house. My sister went into our bedroom where the EMTs had worked on him. She came out and asked what I wanted to do with the jacket they'd cut from his body in order to bare his heart.

"Just get rid of the fucking jacket!" I snarled. The lid was loosening.

"You mean throw it away?" my sister asked, stunned.

A few days later, as we prepared for Roy's funeral, my sister and niece were in our bedroom with me, shuffling through the stacks of books and papers that always cluttered up his bedside stand. We were looking for something, I don't remember what. I pulled open a drawer and stumbled onto his current journal. Like an unsuspecting driver encountering the headlights of a sudden collision, I opened to a page and began to read. The grief hit me like a labor contraction. Uncontrollable sobs and tremors took over my body. I had to lean against the wall and breathe. The lid was off the bottle.

As an old friend used to say, "Getting in touch with your feelings isn't all it's cracked up to be."

Over the next few months, a torrent of emotional backlog wanted out. The harder I fought to keep it contained, the more overwhelmed I became and the more difficult the emotions got. Roy's death was simply the catalyst. Like the gentle prick that launched my son's arrival into the world. I had to process an unknown amount of stored emotion before I could birth my true self into the world.

In his encounter with Nicodemus, Jesus offered a truth about soul work: getting to know the constructed-self, letting it go, and birthing the true self was a requirement. Nicodemus probably had a gut instinct, as I did, that he was running from something. Nicodemus might have suspected that Jesus would lead him to confront the true source of his fears. I don't think it was a purely intellectual exercise for Nicodemus—his soul's longing brought him out in the night.

But, as with the beautiful moment of my son being freed from my womb into the light of our world, the tumult of emotional release and confrontation with the constructed-self disentangled me from a web of illusions. Illusions that created emotions keeping me from sensing the work of Spirit in my life. Much of what I based my constructed-self on was, in fact, an illusion.

Author Caroline Pearson says, "Most of us are slaves of the stories we unconsciously tell ourselves about our lives. Freedom begins the moment we become conscious of the plotline we are living and, with this insight, recognize that we can step into another story altogether."

And yet I lived daily according to the stories, true or not, I'd chosen to believe about my life. As long as I allowed them to operate from an unconscious place, I didn't have a choice about actualizing them. But once I stepped into awareness, I found the freedom to release the ones I no longer wanted to live with. I could write a new story.

The primary illusion I struggled with was separation. Isolation. In her book *Daring Greatly,* sociologist Brené Brown calls this shame. She describes shame as the fear of disconnection or not feeling worthy of connection.

Shame drove me to construct all kinds of aspects of my "self" in order to be protected from disconnection. Like, for example, smiling and going along with the group. This sense of disconnection, I was learning, was really just an illusion as I grew to understand connection as my divine right.

When I clung to illusions strongly enough, I swam in old, protective thoughts and behaviors rather than seeing them for what they were. A constant, subtle fear kept me in fight-or-flight mode, which, in turn, created chronic fatigue. Even though I lived a life of physical safety, when I lived from my constructed-self, I didn't feel safe. Fear, fueled by this illusion, morphed into an incurable sense of responsibility about everything, which activated a need to control.

Working in Roy's business in the years before his death gave me ample opportunity to see some of my illusions play out. When I worked with customers' problems, trying to manage their emotional response and hear their view of the situation, I often felt frustrated and exasperated.

One day, I sat in Roy's office near tears, but still raising my voice to him in anger. He sat back in his chair (probably a blowback from the heated fumes I blasted him with) and got a little parental, as he did when I exasperated him.

"Christine," he said, bringing his fingertips together in a steeple. "You have to remember—when it comes to insurance, you know more than they do."

Growing up with a strongly opinionated father, I learned early and frequently to cross-check my perspective of reality. Like when, at about eight years old, I yelled, "You've gotta help!" at a friend as she left our front porch, meaning she needed to help me clean up the toys before she left.

My father, though, punished me for what he heard me say: "You go to hell." He gave me no opportunity to clarify. I laugh now when I think about my father's horror at hearing his daughter shouting through the neighborhood, "You go to hell!"

In my adolescence, my father's strong need to be correct frequently overshadowed my struggle to express new ideas and opinions. He'd correct me so frequently that I learned to question my perceptions. Hardwired into my nervous system was a fight-or-flight response when others challenged anything I said.

That fear of being wrong or making a mistake created an illusion of instability, even when it came to my expertise. It sent me into panic and confusion where I could no longer think clearly. I started to notice a little habit Roy had developed. When customers sat across the desk from him and challenged his recommendations, he'd sit back, steeple his hands in front of his chest, and click his tongue against the roof of his mouth. Just for a few seconds. He was calming himself and thinking. This pause often settled the customer and changed the energy of the encounter. (It may have also been his therapist training coming into play.)

Unchecked, my fight-or-flight pattern led to toxic emotions such as anger, cynicism, resentment, and bitterness. My mind created all kinds of fears and made elaborate back-up plans in order to feel safe. I'd developed a sophisticated way to hide my vulnerability, but the constant, undergirding vigilance exhausted me.

Spinning plates. The only way out of the constructed-self was to be aware of it. By observing behaviors that didn't serve me, I could make different choices. I could become aware of my soul, my spiritual self, and my connection to Divine Love. I could be born again.

The invitation to connect was always there, but my constructed-self didn't attune to it. Only the true self, the soul, could. In my reading, I was introduced to the concept of vibrational energy. Each person's energy vibrated at different levels, the highest being love. As my constructed-self moved out of the way, the vibration of my soul connected with Divine Love. Mystics called this experience an awakening, an opening to a new level of spiritual experience. My attempts to connect with Divine Love weren't like that. Instead, I liked to think of them as a spiritual "quickening," to stay with Jesus's birthing metaphor. Quickening, as defined in the Oxford English Dictionary, means "to arouse, stimulate, stir, or, as in a pregnancy, to begin to show signs of life, as a fetus in the womb." Jesus used this most basic human experience to draw people into spiritual understanding.

Spiritually, the corollary was awakening to the experience of love. Wise teachers in my life suggested that when I gained a heightened awareness of love, I would start to see it all around me. As this spiritual quickening occurred, experiences looked and felt different. My nervous system calmed down and I could feel my emotions more confidently.

Eventually, my grief experience began to include moments when I looked out my window and gasped at the beauty of the crisp winter light flashing on the snow. I noticed when one of my kids looked up at me and we connected. I became aware of the heightened sensitivity of my soul in the world.

When Nicodemus told Jesus that a man couldn't enter a second time into his mother's womb and be born, I imagined he knew that Jesus was talking about something different, and he wanted to understand it. I don't think he was arguing with Jesus so much as wanting to understand this radical idea.

Jesus went on to say to Nicodemus, "He who believes in Him is not judged," or, as I translated it, "Hey, I'm not here to judge you. I'm here to point you to love."

But the ego, with its dirty little secrets, doesn't want to be exposed. My ego believed exposing the precious, well-kept secrets about who I was in this world, those identities and their defenses, would destroy me. And even if the exposure didn't destroy me, the shame would. Better to keep it all under wraps. The light of truth was a bit too illuminating.

To be present with the truth of me, I needed extravagant love and acceptance. I wasn't satisfied just knowing about this love; I wanted to feel it. What was the experience of feeling unconditionally loved and accepted? It happened, and gradually expanded, for me each time a person chose to be present to my experience, as a light that brought something scary or shameful to the surface.

I didn't want to be the person who, triggered by angry customers, ended up in tears in her husband's office. I wanted to be the confident, competent manager, deftly spinning all the plates. Grief brought those weaknesses to my awareness in a way I could no longer resist. It was a gift: seeing and accepting the flaws I'd tried so hard to keep hidden was my opening to healing.

Each shameful memory, brought to light, was a baby step toward letting go of negative energy. Each letting go opened more space for the energy of the Holy Spirit, and with it came peace, love, and joy. As my prayers transformed from petitions to contemplations, I loosened my stranglehold on my compulsion to problem-solve. My own solutions, outlined for God in desperate entreaties, were nothing more than an ongoing response to fear embedded in the constructed-self.

Perhaps if I let go of that self, my perceived problems would show themselves as illusions. Perhaps I could bear with them and watch them solve themselves, or, better yet, watch Love solve them for me. Or in spite of me. Or even, gasp, without requiring my intervention at all.

Like birth, the process was both natural and miraculous, ferocious and freeing.

THE WELL

Roy and I were neck and neck in a fierce game of Scrabble. Kids sleeping soundly, pizza crusts and empty beer mugs set aside, we approached the end, when all those useless vowels were left over, the juicier consonants having long found homes in obscure words. And then, there it was. I drew a *v*. A *v*! Added to the *i*, *e*, *m*, and *a* I had, if I could find a lonely *n* on the board, I could make the word "Vietnam." (For you Scrabble purists, we cheated and used proper nouns.)

I searched the board and there it was: a letter *n* hanging out over the edge of a word, giving me my opening. I counted the spaces while Roy pondered his next move. It fit! I would be able to use "Vietnam." My victory in the game was nearly secured.

And then … you guessed it. He used the *n*. I looked down at my little tray of letters: "Vietam." A reaction of both humor and anger came over me. I thought I was being funny when I picked up the board and all the letters slid to the middle. But as I tossed it all in the air, I realized I was acting like a child. Roy was laughing. And then he wasn't. The disproportionate anger behind the action surprised us both. It was a fissure in the well-lacquered façade covering a lifetime of disappointments and failures.

Several years later, Roy was diagnosed with an early stage melanoma on his foot. Recovery from the essential surgery put him out of commission as I single-handedly prepared for the family road trip to my parents' lake home. I spent a full Saturday running errands, packing for two children and myself, getting road-trip food ready, loading the car and the rooftop carrier, and taking care of Roy in his state of limited mobility. By the evening before our departure, I was spent and frustrated at having to do everything myself. Roy didn't seem to notice—maybe confronting his own mortality had pushed his focus inward. Regardless, I had little compassion for his existential angst. It was a back-to-back night in our bed.

The next morning, he somehow managed, in his clunky post-surgical boot, to fix me a small tray of tea and toast and clomp his way upstairs to serve me in bed. My cranky mood had not been diminished by a restless night's sleep, and I wanted to have it out. I felt he was trying to cover up the situation by bringing me little gifts rather than dealing with my feelings. I confronted him. He sat on the bed next to me, hefted his leg up, and tried to listen. Then he defended. And I defended. We both knew the kids would be waking soon and it would be time to get on the road.

Tension built as the pattern of defense and accusation we'd honed over ten years of marriage made its way into our conversation yet again. I looked hard at him as, in one swift gesture, I picked up the breakfast tray and threw it against the closet. Pottery shattered and tea splashed the closet door, dripping to the floor. This wasn't a Scrabble board.

He got up off the bed and limped out of the bedroom. Not missing a beat, I threw the blankets aside and moved into preparation mode, leaving with the kids shortly after, the anger still hanging in the air between us.

Overwhelm. Frustration. Anger.

Shame.

The wardrobe of my constructed-self.

We all have strategies for meeting our needs. This reminded me of the woman Jesus encountered at a well in a small town called Samaria. Jesus, a Jew, was resting at the well, the central fixture in the town. Samaritans were hostile to Jews—about a hundred years earlier, the Jewish high priest had destroyed their temple. Bad blood still existed. So, when Jesus asked a Samaritan woman to draw him water to drink, she was taken aback. Not only was it unusual for a man to speak to a woman he didn't know, but it was also forbidden for Jews to use anything in common with Samaritans.

She queried Jesus about why he should be asking her for a drink.

He said to her, "If you know the gift of God and who is saying to you, 'Give me a drink,' you would have asked him, and he would have given you living water."

Like Nicodemus, the woman was disoriented as Christ moved her into the realm of the sacred. She, too, brought out the rational defenses, saying that since Jesus didn't have a bucket and the well was quite deep, she wondered how he expected to find water.

There at the well, in a mundane daily ritual and casual encounter, Jesus opened the door for a different kind of exchange. He interacted from a spiritual plane, and she pushed back from her material experience. She invoked her tribal story of an ancestral patriarch, saying, "You are not greater than our father Jacob, are you, who gave us the well and drank of it himself, and his sons, and his cattle?"

She went on the defense and drew on her intellect. The woman knew her history. She took a position. In the flash of a moment, she engaged in a survival exercise used by women throughout time: she formulated her response to another male threat. But she was disoriented. He was talking about something she couldn't relate to, a living water, a wellspring of life. Jesus looked past her defenses and into her heart. He knew, somehow, that she was longing for something in the same way a thirsty person longed for a dipper of water.

Jesus told her to call her husband, and she answered that she had no husband. He replied that she'd spoken well—he knew she'd had five husbands, and that the man she was currently with was not her husband.

As a young Christian, I learned some pretty shaming and damning interpretations of this scripture. There existed in my religious community a deep-seated suspicion of women who couldn't keep a husband. To the ministers and lay leaders of my youth, the woman in this story deceptively hid the truth of her life. She was so lost and full of sin that she'd been through no less than four husbands, and now she wasn't even married to the man she called her husband. My community misinterpreted her deep-seated need for connection and protection as promiscuity, and chalked it up to a moral failure.

I saw her differently.

I saw myself in this woman. Only by degrees was she less liberated than I. Two thousand years later, women still live in a culture where misogyny, discrimination, and dismissive attitudes prevail. I admit I was initially tempted to agree with my earlier teachers; to see her with condescension as a poor, young, uneducated village woman struggling to keep a husband. But as I considered how my own needs drove my choices, I saw her through a different lens.

If this woman had been through four husbands and was living with a fifth, she had some experience under her belt. I didn't see her as young, ignorant, and confused. I saw a strong but softened woman, wise in her silence but thoughtful and curious in her interactions. Neither did I see Jesus as a condescending patriarchal figure ready to ruthlessly expose and shame her for having five husbands. Instead, I saw Jesus offering her compassion and healing.

I imagined two adults finding their way into an intimate conversation. She appeared very forthright. She said, You're a Jew. Why are you asking me for water?

And then Jesus started to bring up these strange ideas about living water.

It made me see Jesus's vulnerability. He kept trying to reveal himself to people, but it made them uncomfortable. Like Nicodemus. Like this woman.

So, why did Jesus talk to her? He longed to ease her suffering, but he needed to get past her intellectual defenses. Because those defenses blocked the gateways in her spirit from which living water was meant to flow.

My own defenses worked as rigid ramparts to stem the flow of emotions I didn't want to feel. But allowing those emotions—the living water, the energy—to flow and be released through my body was the only way to ease my suffering. I saw how I, too, operated when something came into my life and threatened to touch a vulnerable place, a hidden part of myself, suggesting I might feel the related emotion. I'd deflect by trying to figure it out. I'd get intellectual and analytical.

Like the woman at the well, when Roy died, I drew on all the learning I'd gained, the wisdom of my tribe, and the research available to make sense of what happened. And I learned, as this woman did, that it wasn't possible to reason my way into a spiritual connection with the Divine. In his desire to lead people into their own hearts, Jesus blew the hinges off their doors of protection. What rang true in this encounter was the intimacy of this woman's exposure; the vulnerability of her emotional experience. How she pushed back from her intellect but ultimately came to a place of trust.

Of course, it wasn't wrong to use my mind to understand my world and make decisions about my actions and relationships. But this alone didn't satisfy my need to be seen and validated. I wasn't ready to acknowledge my longings, let alone experience them. To do so demanded a level of trust in Divine Love I had not yet known.

Before Roy died, I'd been pretty confident arguing and finger-pointing my way through anything that threatened to expose my vulnerabilities. But my intellectual defense was a house of cards—when I found myself without a partner to carry the weight of my projections, it collapsed.

This started with my attempts to "figure out" the grieving process. I approached it like a thesis project. I read all the experts, underlined key notes and quotes, but absorbed nothing. I stalked Facebook grieving groups, dutifully participated in an in-person grief group, and slowly moved through my to-do list for the bereaved. There wasn't anything wrong with my process. It just couldn't help me accept the emotions that entered my house when death knocked and demanded a seat at my hearth.

Another version of my defense system was believing that if I could fix a problem, I wouldn't feel the pain of it. When we went to therapy as a family and one of the kids would cry about an issue, I would open the dialogue to "figure out" what prompted the tears. Empathy wasn't my strong suit. One day, one of the kids was angry and crying. The therapist looked at me and almost imperceptibly tilted her head toward my child, suggesting I extend some comfort. My child wanted a gentle touch. A reassuring hug.

When my twenty-four-year-old son came home at 2:00 a.m. three days after Roy's death and sat across from me weeping, struggling with the brutal reality that he would never see his father again, no amount of intellectualizing would comfort or soothe him. Here was a problem I would never be able to fix. I could only reach out to this now grown man, invite him into my overstuffed chair, snuggle his head against my shoulder, and cry with him.

The moment of being broken open, whether through my own suffering or watching the suffering of my children, left me so vulnerable that it was terrifying to stay present. But staying present in emotion—"sitting with it," as I've heard since—was my pathway to healing. This bearing with suffering was my greatest challenge. Occasionally, someone would offer the advice to "keep busy" as an anecdote to grief, as though the momentum of constant movement and mental distraction would somehow get me through the anguish. Embedded there was the belief that to sit with negative emotion was to risk wallowing—a very slippery slope. And who wants to do that anyway? But I found the practice of bearing with my suffering to be unavoidable. Necessary. Healing. A basic building block for resilience. And, truth be told, I didn't have a lot of energy for "keeping busy."

As he continued to talk with the Samaritan woman, Jesus gently confronted her intellectual protections. I imagined him going through his spiritual Rolodex, sifting for the right thing to say, the opening to her guarded spirit. The gentle touch. Therapists the world over should exclaim in awe at how Jesus paid attention to this woman. How he used his intuition to perceive her need and find the best action or word to draw her closer to her truth.

Jesus was both extraordinarily perceptive and incomparably compassionate. His focus was not on how he could control and manipulate this woman in order to make himself feel important, but how he could help her open up to love. I don't think he knew what was going to transpire in every interaction he had with people. I do think he knew, really clearly, what he was about.

He chose to touch on the most sensitive aspect of her spirit. What had happened in this woman's life? She was with her fifth man and wasn't married to him. Where others saw promiscuity and sin, Jesus saw her longing. Then, he gently helped her see it.

I couldn't see into the wounded places in my spirit without a gentle and compassionate guide. Like the woman at the well, I looked at Jesus and said, "Wait, you mean you know this about me? You see my deep longing, my raging anger, my coping defenses? You mean I don't have to hide from it anymore? I don't want to know this about myself because I couldn't stand the pain, the shame, or the guilt. How is it you know? How is it you accept me?" The compassion Jesus offered her showed me it was okay to be wounded. It was okay to hurt. It was okay to be vulnerable. It was even okay to rage, appropriately. Constantly defending myself against truth—and running from it—was what destroyed my peace and wore me out.

I suspected that Jesus repeatedly broke through the religious taboos about women because he knew that the embodiment of God must also be received and expressed in a way unique to them—the patriarchal religious institution of his time offered little opportunity for a feminine expression of Divine Love. He knew he would find respect and wonder and openness once he built trust in the hearts of women.

First, he told her who she was.

Then he told her who he was.

Then he invited her to let go of her constructed-self in order to find her true self.

I imagined the moment between them after Jesus revealed her truth. Her soul was laid bare. She conceded that she was talking with a prophet. Jesus gently told her about spirit and truth. She inched toward it. She looked at him hard. Longingly. Expectantly.

She said, "I know the messiah is coming. He will tell us what's going on."

Jesus looked at her and said, "I who speak to you am he."

Then disciples showed up and the moment was over. They were all hustle-bustle and "let's get Jesus some food." I imagined Jesus remaining very present with her, watching her walk away as the disciples vied for his attention.

The woman had been touched. Her longing had not only been revealed, but respected and validated. Jesus had sent a message: I know your longing; I know your suffering. I see it. I see you.

I could only connect with the parts of myself I was willing to see. I could only explore my interior world when I trusted the ground beneath my feet and offered myself compassion and forgiveness. Otherwise it was too shameful. Too exposed. Too vulnerable. But once revealed, those nasty bits began to give way to something else.

I saw how the energy of shame, guilt, and self-loathing filled up space in my spirit. When I released it and allowed it to move, something else filled those spaces: light, as an experience. Love, as the filling of my heart. A friend once told me that after her husband died, she felt like every nerve ending in her body was exposed. She could feel not only her own raw emotions, but also the emotions of those around her. Everything was so intense, and not just the grief—also the love and joy.

Grief opened me up to this intensity, and at times, I felt the love so strongly that I almost couldn't take it. When a spirit, an energy so holy, so purely love, filled the spaces between my cells, the very energy of my being transformed.

Living water.

Franciscan monk Richard Rohr wrote of this process in his weekly blog in 2017: "True liberation is letting go of our small self, letting go of our cultural biases, and letting go of our fear of loss and death. Freedom is letting go of wanting more and better things, and it is letting go of our need to control and manipulate God and others. It is even letting go of our need to know and our need to be right—which we only discover with maturity. We become free as we let go of our three primary energy centers: our need for power and control, our need for safety and security, and our need for affection and esteem."

"It wasn't a big deal," Jesus seemed to say to the woman. "About the five husbands. I didn't bring it up to make you feel bad. I brought it up because it showed me the pathway into your wound." He invited her to open the wound to the light, to see her true self and let the healing energy move; to be awakened to the healing moments and let the living water flow.

I've never understood why this was the way healing worked. But it seemed to be. Deep suffering, when seen and embraced, opened my soul. It was gut-wrenching; not for the weak of heart. Should you find yourself entering into this experience, go gently and with great self-compassion.

THE POOL

AFTER A LITTLE OVER THREE MONTHS OF GRIEVING, the Fourth of July came parading in, the first holiday to catch my attention. Morning anxiety woke me as the effects of my sleep medication ebbed away. I looked at the clock. 4:00 a.m. I calculated over sixteen hours until fireworks. I counted back. My daughter had invited me for dinner. We would meet at 6:00 p.m. Fourteen hours. I desperately needed a shower. Thirteen hours before I really had to get out of bed. I could cancel. I rolled over and tried to find oblivion in sleep. It would not come.

Throwing the sheets aside, I considered another sleeping pill: eight hours' worth of uninterrupted peace. I had time. But instead, I padded the ten feet to my bathtub, watched the water rush in for a long time and then padded back to the bookshelf in my room to make a selection from my growing library of grief memoirs. I returned to the tub, turned off the water. I opened a bottle of lavender oil and watched the slow drips, one, two, three, four, five, drop into the steaming bath. A cup of Epsom salts. Easing myself into the womb-like warmth, I let the saltwater of still more tears mingle with the water in the tub.

I chose to try *The Grief Recovery Handbook* again. Its subtitle was *The Action Program for Moving Beyond Death, Divorce, and Other Losses including Health, Career, and Faith.*

That just about covers everything, I thought cynically. I read and soaked ... and then I had an epiphany. People died from grief. It was possible I could, too. Grief recovery wouldn't just happen to me—it was something I had to make happen. I cried some more about the overwhelming unknown and my part in it.

Forced out by the cooling water, I stepped from the bathtub and into my standing shower. I turned the hot water up to searing and washed my hair like I hadn't washed it in months. I scrubbed my skin with a loofah sponge. I got out and sat with conditioner in my hair for an hour, then washed it out and wove a braid. Makeup. A summer dress and sandals, selected from my closet. I made and ate a sandwich.

This entire process took about four hours. By the time I sat in my favorite chair, shoring up the courage to return to the exercises in the grief workbook, I trembled with fatigue.

As summer heat turned to cool evening, I ate a hot dog with my daughter and somewhat enjoyed the fireworks. Returning home, I poured a scotch to take out to the deck. Lights twinkled over my neighbor's patio and I heard the soft music and muted conversation of a party. And then I remembered: it was the annual Fourth of July gathering we often shared with neighbors. I hadn't been invited. The sting of rejection reminded me, again, how hard it was all going to be.

I felt like the man Jesus encountered by the pool at Bethesda. In the story, Jesus came upon a sick man lying by a pool of water known to have sacred healing properties. When the water in the pool stirred, those who entered were healed. The man was too broken to get himself into the pool, and his suffering seemed to be exacerbated by watching as the ripples moved through and no one offered to help him reach them.

I was that man. I was waiting for something magical to end my grief. I'd read stories about people who said they just woke up one day and it was gone, like a miraculous clearing. That was not me.

I imagined the five roofed porches surrounding the pool, peopled by a sick, blind, lame, and withered group who had nowhere else to go. Society's rejects. I imagined the stench was overpowering and conversation a strain. Despair permeated the air where people waited for the mystical stirring of water to change their lives. The lost, the forgotten, the desperate.

Jesus approached the man and said to him, "Do you wish to get well?"

Of course a person who'd been ill for thirty-eight years would want to get well. But as I considered the question for my own life, I wondered if there wasn't some critical truth about the human relationship with the Divine embedded in the story. Something about human agency, desire, longing, participation, and trust all wrapped up into one question: "Do you want to get well?"

Ongoing wellness, as with everything in the universe, was a living, breathing, changing, transforming, nurturing, growing, and dying process. To choose spiritual healing meant embarking on a process of stripping away all that was not God. We all wanted to be healed, did we not? It wasn't a question of desire. The question was, Did I want to do the work to bring about healing?

Well, of course. And hell no.

So, it seemed kind of Jesus to ask.

Sipping my scotch on the deck, I entertained a few questions. Did I want to open to the process of shedding anything keeping me from being well—anything blocking my access to Love? Did I want to take initiative and engage my agency? Was I ready to let go of my self-limiting victim mentality and behaviors? Could I imagine alternative responses to suffering?

In his book *On Growth and Form*, mathematician D'Arcy Wentworth Thompson says that it's "a very important physiological truth that a condition of strain, the result of a stress, is a direct stimulus to growth itself. ... The soles of our boots wear thin, but the soles of our feet grow thick the more we walk upon them: for it would seem that living cells are "stimulated" by pressure."

Perhaps the same principle applied to spiritual experience. Could I see my suffering as a condition of strain or stress that could lead to growth?

When Jesus encountered the sick man, he told him the same thing I realized that evening on my deck: if I was going to find my way through grief, I couldn't wait around for someone or something magical to make it happen. I had to get up, put one foot in front of the other, and move forward. Or at least in the direction of forward.

Even so, I do remember that Fourth of July as a magical day. The day I shifted in grief from feeling like a victim to finding some agency in my healing.

From my new perspective, Jesus's respect for the sick man's power to choose whether he wanted to get well created a spiritual opening for me. Divine Consciousness had created me with this agency, this potential for growth.

In my rag-bag of old beliefs, the image of God as an external power pulling the strings in my life was the first casualty. That illusion may have created a false sense of security, but along with it came limitation and frustration. I had unwittingly agreed to a patriarchal bargain that went something like this: "you participate in our relationship the way I want you to and I will protect and provide for you." It was tempting because I thought I needed a cosmic bodyguard to care for me—and a cosmic authority figure to blame and shake my finger at when all did not go well. Unfortunately, this bargain had meant abdicating my agency and responsibility.

The man by the pool had also abdicated his agency. He believed he was out of options—that something outside of him both had to happen and kept it from happening. He'd been lying by the pool for thirty-eight years, and yet Jesus showed him something within himself that enabled him to get up and walk. But where did he go? How did he continue to live his life?

I'd sampled this concept of agency when I attended Burning Man. One of the ten principles of the festival's founding group was "radical self-reliance." My son and I decided to travel together but stay in separate camps, so I lived in the desert community for one week, responsible primarily for and to myself. At the end of the week, after the final night of revelry, my son and I cued up in a long line of vehicles making the slow exodus from camp. It took most of the night to leave the site and drive the 120 miles to our interim hotel in Reno before making the journey home. The blinking lights and noise of the slot machines in the hotel casino were a shock to my system after a week in the desert.

Whenever we traveled together, Roy, being the gentleman he was, carried my bags. But when Burning Man was over and Sam and I arrived at the hotel, Roy wasn't there. I was exhausted and hungry and filthy with playa dust, and not terribly happy about the weight of my pack. I let it fall to the ceramic-tiled floor of the registration line, shuffling it forward with my foot as we progressed.

When it was our turn, I looked pleadingly at my son to carry my bag the short distance to the counter. He raised one eyebrow, half-smiling, the way Roy did. "Radical self-reliance," he said. I shuffled my bag up to the registration desk, but I didn't carry it a step farther. Instead, I tipped the bellman.

After Roy died, I learned how to stain a deck, repair a broken fence, fix a garbage disposal, use a lawnmower and a snow blower … and dry my own tears. I also learned to ask for help when tasks felt bigger than me, like replacing the garage door opener, building a new fence, and carrying my bag at the end of a long journey.

The illusion of victimization was embedded in my grief experience. Being wounded felt like being victimized. Yes, something had been taken away from me or imposed upon me and it was outside of my control. But how I responded to and lived with the suffering was where the illusion needed to melt away.

My victim illusion sounded like this: I can't live with that. I shouldn't have to live with that. I don't want to live with that. Or my personal favorite, How come they get to rush into the pool when it's astir and I can't?

To confront the illusion, I instead asked, What am I waiting for? Whose permission am I seeking? Who do I think is going to pick me up and put me in the pool? I thought about how much of my creative energy was taken up with negative emotions anchoring me to the past.

And so, Jesus said, pick up your mat and walk.

Yes, I could live with it. I might not think I deserved to, and I might not want to, but I could, and I would. It was a tough one. I didn't want to take lightly the horrors of what some people carried. At times, the suffering of others was so great that I instinctively looked away.

At a cursory glance, it looked easy for Jesus when, miraculously, the man did indeed pick up his mat and walk. But the story continued. After the healing, Jesus slipped away. He didn't want to be recognized by the challenging authorities (the same ones who, by the way, confronted the healed man and told him he couldn't carry his mat because it was the sabbath). But even though Jesus had an exit strategy, he wasn't finished. Wanting to connect with the man, Jesus sought him out later in the temple. "Stop doing this to yourself," Jesus said to him, "so nothing worse will happen to you."

The healing opportunity ran deeper. To Jesus's suggestion I had to ask, Stop doing what? The answers I offered myself were: stop living as a victim, stop waiting for others to make it happen for you, stop living a disconnected life. Healing may have begun with a seismic quaking of my spirit, but it continued in a million momentary shifts.

As I picked up my suffering and began walking into the journey of grief, I encountered a myriad of unexpected changes I had to make in my life, from the profound to the mundane. One day, my "occupational grief therapist" Kendra and I headed over to Toys "R" Us to pick out a baby fence for my aging Yorkshire terrier. She was becoming incontinent, and I decided to keep her in a confined space.

Kendra and I stood in front of the row of options, and I plunged into my decision-making chatter. "I don't think that one will be big enough. And that one, ugh, it just looks like ropes, right?"

She'd try to respond, but I just talked over her. I continued my banter and then realized her silence. I was used to Roy's well-timed responses, rehearsed over a thirty-three-year marriage. She just stood there and stared at me.

"Do you want me to answer?" she asked.

As I paused to consider her comment, I realized I was trying to make decisions with Kendra in the same way I had with Roy. When we collaborated on a purchase, we'd banter back and forth about size, price, quality, whatever, until we somehow reached a decision. Kendra didn't know how to play our game. I stood in front of the baby gates and choked back tears, realizing I would never make decisions with him again. One tiny change. A monumental shift.

A myriad of small changes invited me to connect deeply with my felt experience. Choosing presence in the face of tumultuous change required courage. I saw my fear of unknown possibilities reflected in the religious leaders' response to the sick man's healing. When confronted with the inexplicable, they defaulted to legalities. They told him he couldn't carry his mat on the sabbath, a day when work of any kind was forbidden. "Who gave you permission to behave this way?" they asked.

The Jewish establishment's attempt to maintain the status quo reminded me of my constructed-self. My ego held onto thought patterns and behaviors that maintained the illusion of safety. Each time I opened myself to an experience of deep feeling, I risked the stability of my well-crafted, confident, competent self.

But what I thought was at risk—my crafted stability—was really just rickety scaffolding obscuring my authentic self. As I let it fall, dismantling its defenses, I learned to create a genuine sense of confidence; one built from my own engagement with trying, failing, surrendering, and recovering. Or trying, succeeding, and still surrendering and recovering. I practiced inviting emotions in and trusting my ability to return to balance.

I found agency in the trying. In the failing. But I had to balance it with surrender, because agency without surrender could become as unstable as Icarus's wings. This mythological man who flew too close to the sun and melted the wax of his handmade wings offered a warning. As I explored moving into the emotions of my grief, I needed to notice when agency turned to overreaching and required the comforting release of surrender. Because nothing went as planned.

Many times in my journey toward healing, I felt forward movement and then slid back into despair—like the July evening when I encountered my victim self. When I discovered that I'd been excluded from the neighbor's party, I needed to feel the agency of my ability to heal, but I also needed to entertain the invitation to surrender. My emotions needed a loving observer, not a demanding drill sergeant. For both the woman at the well and the man by the pool, Jesus offered radical grace. I wanted to invite grace into my relationship with myself.

The Divine was always present with me and within me as a loving observer, but I struggled to access the love. Grief, anger, and despair were too strong or scary. When I felt overwhelmed, I needed help. I needed a wise person to stand in for the Divine and keep me present with the emotions until I found my internal connection to safely observe and love the full range of feelings.

Even, or maybe especially, when my heart shattered, I learned to experience a fuller spectrum of emotions. When the pain was severe and I didn't have the confidence of past experience to guide me, I sought help from trusted guides who had journeyed the path before me. I watched a new beauty emerge. I'd assumed that a heart broken into fragments left a void, like a vessel no longer able to hold what it was meant to—a vulnerable opening, a brokenness beyond repair. My fears dissipated as this space, rather than contracting, opened out. What I thought would be emptiness, a garden decimated in a hailstorm, instead expanded into a lush new landscape. To a larger, fuller experience.

If I could find the courage to be present with pain, to feel the fluttering in my gut, the heaviness in my heart, the trembling in my hands, then the energy could move and transform into something else.

Healing appeared in my willingness to dance with the cosmos, to co-create my responses to daily moments. How would I respond when a sock hiding in the laundry, a photograph, or just a mention of Roy provoked wrenching pain, despair, frustration, guilt, shame, or terror? Who would I choose to be when encountering Love that confronted my excuses and sent light through my wall of protection? How would I live, broken open to everything I'd tried to avoid? How would I pick up my mat and walk?

In his talk with the paralyzed man, Jesus suggested, "Don't sin anymore," which I took to mean, "Don't hide anymore."

I imagined Jesus saying, You don't have to separate yourself from me out of fear and guilt and shame. You are deeply connected to me. The scaffolding you built around yourself is no longer necessary. You can begin to dismantle it, if you choose. If you want to heal.

On the many days when I woke up feeling despair, or shame, I learned to pick up the mat of my suffering, see it, walk with it, and bring the metals of my emotions to the spiritual alchemy this message promised. I chose Love. Love chose me. We walked. And in my very best moments, when I was brave in my heart and open to the light and love longing to find me and fill my being, we danced.

THE FEAST

IN 1986, MY PARENTS CELEBRATED their thirtieth wedding anniversary. I decided the event deserved a party. A grand party. Being a romantic, I thought it should be at the Pheasant Run Resort, a hotel in the Chicago suburbs where my parents enjoyed dates during their courtship. It didn't matter to me if nobody in our immediate family lived in Chicago; our extended family was still there, and those folks made up the bulk of the invitation list.

I told the event planner how my parents dated there and were about to celebrate their anniversary. He gave me a meeting room rental for free with a guaranteed food and beverage amount. Each of my three siblings and I donated four hundred dollars. I had $1,600 to create a party for about two hundred people. That's right: eight dollars per person.

Undaunted (and naive), we selected the least expensive appetizers, decided a cash bar would be essential (less alcohol, less drama) and planned some skits, songs, and a slideshow for entertainment. (A real slideshow, with slides in a rotating tray.) A cousin donated his time as the disc jockey. We had a party.

And then, the day before the party, as everyone gathered at the hotel, the magic started to happen. When I checked in with our meeting planner, he said they'd had a cancellation for one of their ballrooms, the one with the stage, and asked whether we would like to move the party in there. Well, heck yeah!

When my father led my mom up to the event room, instead of peering around an unremarkable doorway, they encountered tall, wooden double doors that swung open to the cheers of their entire extended family congratulating them.

When my father discovered the cash bar, he was mortified and slapped down his credit card to cover the drinks. Someone may have also secretly beefed up the appetizer menu because the food somehow made it through the evening. Our skits and humor got a professional bump by being performed onstage. With the generosity of my dad, the grace of family members who appreciated four strapped-for-cash kids doing something nice for their parents, and some hospitality tossed in by the event manager, we had our little miracle.

Later, I learned that my parents had actually never been to the Pheasant Run Resort. The place I saw in those yellowed photos of my mom lolling by the pool was someplace else altogether. Perhaps the angels of mirth had a little chuckle over my attempts at making a miracle. I received it as a blessing, nonetheless.

In the midst of grief, when it felt like everything was gone, when the world turned inside out and the light narrowed to a single pinpoint of searing pain, I tried to access memories of these kinds of little miracles. To believe they still existed. Remembering the abundance of our anniversary celebration reminded me of the story about Jesus feeding thousands with just five loaves of bread and two fish.

As Jesus walked from village to village teaching and preaching, his reputation grew, and so did the crowds who gathered to hear him. One evening, he sat on a hill overlooking the throngs of people. He asked a disciple, Philip, how they might buy bread for everyone. The story told us Jesus's question was a test: "And this he was saying to test him; for he himself knew what he was intending to do." But it didn't say why. I wondered, what was Jesus looking for from Philip? What was the right answer? It seemed like it had something to do with trust.

Philip responded that even if they had two hundred denarii worth of bread, (a denarius being a day's wage) it wouldn't be enough for everyone to receive even a little. Another disciple, Andrew, noticed a boy in the crowd who had two fish and five barley loaves. Jesus told the disciples to have everyone sit on the grass. The story said there were about five thousand people.

"Jesus therefore took the loaves, and having given thanks, he distributed to those who were seated; likewise also of the fish as much as they wanted. And when they were filled, he said to his disciples, 'Gather up the leftover fragments so that nothing may be lost.' And so, they gathered them up and filled twelve baskets with fragments from the five barley loaves which were left over by those who had eaten."

Jesus took what they had, gave thanks, and worked with it. And a miracle happened. I saw a ritual in Jesus's actions. First, he took honest inventory. They only had five loaves of bread and two fishes. Then he blessed it. He gave thanks for what was there, meager as it seemed. Then he encouraged the disciples to take action, to distribute the food. His ritual, incorporated into my daily habits, provided an exercise of gratitude and abundance as I faced the illusion of my spiritual limitations. Like the disciples in this story, I doubted my resources.

Walking with the challenges of grief, I felt like the spiritual nourishment I brought to healing added up to little more than five loaves and two fishes. It felt insufficient. I couldn't draw much from my spiritual inheritance as the great-granddaughter of German and Norwegian immigrants. My mother was raised in a family where children were to be seen and not heard. If a child spoke at her grandmother's dinner table, they were slapped into silence. As immigrant farmers, my ancestors' lives were shaped by the strict adherence to religious morality infused into day-to-day survival. Not the necessary morality teaching us—in a healthy society—to choose good, compassion, and care; a punishing and limiting morality requiring adherence to ill-considered rules.

My own parents created a more compassionate home environment for us, but our days were filled with the schedule of modern life: school, activities, two working parents, lots of busyness with little time or space for emotion and personal reflection. As a grade-school child and early adolescent, I found my way to singing in the church choir and connecting with church youth groups, following a yearning for something I didn't know existed. I felt reverence in the sanctuary of my family church, the sheen on the dark wood pews, the light filtering in through stained glass, the echoes of anthems reverberating from the choir loft. I felt safe.

But I had no idea how to translate my Sunday experience into daily life. Spiritually, I was fed at the table of patriarchal Christianity, with its focus on laws and meritocracy. The demands of conformity and performance did little to feed my soul's longing for connection and acceptance. When led into the transition grief forced on me, I looked into a spiritual void and said, I can't do this. I don't have what it takes.

At times, taking inventory, counting the loaves and fishes, meant nothing more than saying I didn't know. When I couldn't stay present in that liminal space of unknowing, I cast around for someone to help me make sense of my experience. Earlier in my life, when I grappled with the awful feeling of sliding down a slippery slope and losing control, a wise woman told me to just sit down—that the mental frenzy took me away from God.

The unknowing, when I could be present to it, created the opening to healing.

When faced with their own unknown, the disciples looked to Jesus. But he gave the problem back to them: he asked them where they could buy enough bread for everyone. Perhaps he wanted Philip to be confronted by his limitations.

As I moved, gradually, from my narrowed focus to something larger, I saw my own limitations by comparison. My overwhelming, embarrassing, vulnerable, powerless limitations. For Philip, the task of feeding five thousand people meant acknowledging limitations and stepping into the unknown. I liked to imagine that Jesus knew the disciples wouldn't have an answer to their dilemma, but he wanted to give them the opportunity to experience their human limitations before they saw the possibility of expanding into spiritual abundance. In this way, the trauma of Roy's death brought me into a void that opened my spirit to learning about gratitude and abundance. One day, one moment at time.

The day Roy died, the blessed company of family members who sat with me into my first dark night sustained me. At three or four o'clock in the morning, the last friend succumbed to fatigue and suggested sleep. I stepped into the bedroom for the first time since the paramedics had turned our nest of thirty-three years into a chaotically constructed operating theater.

I sat on the bed and noticed the birthday card Roy had given me just two days earlier, haphazardly tossed onto my nightstand with a few other greetings. I picked it up, and as I opened it, my body moved out of the numbness of those first hours to shock. I experienced my first major bout of trembling while reading the prophetic message, a Marcus Aurelius quote: "When you arise in the morning, think of what a privilege it is to be alive: to breathe, to think, to enjoy, to love."

Later, I framed it and set it on my nightstand so I would see it first thing each day. Some mornings I turned it face down. Other mornings I wanted to throw it across the room. With loss hanging like a dark scrim between me and the world, I had to be reintroduced to what remained before I could even consider blessing it.

I no longer had a husband, or a job, or the business we worked in together. I no longer had my friend, lover, confidant, cook, repairman, or partner. I no longer had the stability of a structured day in an office where phones rang and problems were solved. I no longer had my source of comfort as I drifted off to sleep, or my grounding when I stirred each morning.

Over time, as I woke to see my birthday card, I felt Roy reminding me what life was really about. Breathing, thinking, enjoying, loving—they all became items in my gratitude inventory; the loaves and fishes that helped me get out of bed on many days.

I had to remind myself that it was a privilege to be alive. I started with rising out of sleep and into consciousness each morning. My inventory wasn't always pretty, but I tried to bless my waking and gave thanks. I feel like shit, I thought, but I'm awake and alive. I'm breathing. Thank you for breath.

Other days, I would think, I feel like shit, so at least I can feel something. Thank you. Thank you for my emotions and how they shape my life even when they don't feel good.

My soul cracked open a fraction, and I considered the experience of trust. Like a starving person smelling food, I was quickened by the sense of possibility. Limiting experiences could be reframed into self-awareness. New awareness came more easily with a gentle receptivity reminding me that whatever I found, no matter how embarrassing or shameful, I could love myself. I could embrace what felt meager and insufficient and begin to trust myself again.

In my deepest suffering, rather than feeling grateful for what I had, I despaired about what I'd lost. And this directed my choices. When I interpreted loss as God taking something away from me, my life shrank. I feared more would be taken away. I clung more tightly. As I moved into abundance, I took inventory and explored the experience of gratitude.

I had somehow arrived at my fifty-seventh year needing to learn about embodied emotional experience. I wasn't consciously thinking, I could use some comfort now, or boy, I'm really longing for some attention. A new type of discernment had to open for me after I started watching myself and interpreting my feelings and needs.

As my defenses peeled away, I sensed something beneath them: longing. In the same way a starving person slowly loses the sensation of hunger, I'd lost my sense of longing. I'd simply stopped feeling any emotional needs. My internal refrain was, No really, I'm fine. I'll take care of it. I've got this.

So, my needs shrunk back into my soul and stopped asking for attention. The space in my heart created for comfort, empathy, connection, and safety filled instead with anger as frustration seeped from my spirit and took up residence in my being.

Once I admitted I had needs, then wants, then longings, then desires, then dreams, I reflected on why I hadn't seen them earlier. Perhaps it was due to a lack of my own attention telling me my needs were okay, normal, and human. A loving, observing, reflecting presence. I discovered I could be that loving presence for myself.

When the ego I had built for survival caused more pain than comfort, I was compelled to turn to something infinitely greater (or even just a tiny bit greater) than my constructed-self. I tried to shush her for a while, sit quietly, and see if something different would happen. I tried allowing a thought or feeling to gently and calmly present itself. Into this opening entered the possibility of abundance.

As the months added up and it had been—unbelievably— nearly a year since Roy's death, I came to a point where I could ponder the question posed regularly by my therapist: "What brings you joy?"

In the demanding life I'd lived, raising two children, working, and fighting for creative time, I hadn't stopped to consider joy. My longing for joy seemed to have taken the same subterranean dive as my other longings. But when despair threatened the comfort of each day, I was presented with an opportunity to move away from my limiting emotions and into a new possibility of abundance.

Around this time, an out-of-town friend invited me to visit her while she helped care for her twin grandsons. Those few days brought me back to my early college life, when I studied education and worked at the campus preschool. It reminded me of the natural joy I often experienced while raising my two kids. I sent a photo of me holding one of the beautiful three-month-old boys to my family and some other friends. Many said that I looked like "my old self." That there was light in my eyes again.

After that, I was able to say to my therapist, "Children. Children bring me joy."

A few months later, it was time for me to go back out into the world to find a job. I called the director of the school my children had attended and asked if she had anything I could do, work or volunteer. She met with me the next day. Two months later, I started working with one-year-olds three days a week.

Nothing demands attention like young children. For three days every week, I spent five hours outside of myself. I didn't have time to think about the scary unknowns of my future. I laughed and smiled at the antics of one-year-olds. I reveled in their longing to attach, to be held and cuddled. I found exceeding joy in each threshold they passed, from walking to communicating with sign language, from babbling to discovering words. I built on small, singular moments of joy until they formed a larger, more consistent expectation and awareness of joy. It was my first experience of cultivating positive emotion with intention.

I used to view the concept of abundance through the lens of material experience. Through that lens, abundance meant a whole lot of whatever I wanted, mostly money so I could be in control and feel safe. Through grief, I learned about spiritual abundance. An abundance of possibilities. An abundance of ideas. An abundance of creative solutions. An abundance of options. An abundance of love, safety, belonging, joy.

When I didn't know what to do, when my future seemed uncertain and I felt frightened, anxious, and overwhelmed, I tried to take inventory of what I did have. My two children figured strongly in this exercise, as did my friends and the new support system I was constructing over time.

I also took spiritual inventory: the creative spirit within me, expressed through writing, painting, and other arts; the mountains in the near distance that embraced me daily like a cosmic hug; my newfound experience with my own emotions and embodied spirituality. I blessed it. I tried to trust that the answers would come and multiply my resources. Trust that the problem didn't need to be solved immediately. Trust in timing. Trust in abundance, in hope and joy and inspiration. Perhaps I wasn't feeling those things in the moment, but maybe I could call up a memory and trust the possibility.

It wasn't easy, this moment-by-moment practice. But when I paused to recognize a loss, fear, yearning, want, desire, or need to be fed in some way—each time I took inventory of what I did have, what I had accomplished, and what I could do—I blessed it and watched for the miracle, perhaps already taking place.

THE MYSTERY

THE DAY ROY DIED, I found myself in the midst of a family reunion, in the deepest state of shock I'd ever experienced. My older sister and brother-in-law were already at the house when my son and I arrived home from the hospital. They drove over and picked up my mom. Then their four adult children arrived, followed by my aunt, cousin, and my younger sister and her six adult children. My brother, who'd visited for my birthday two days earlier, had just arrived home in Austin. He turned around to fly back.

Two of our oldest friends agreed to officiate the funeral together. Roy's old boss and her husband flew in from Oregon, my old boss flew from Minnesota, our kids' old babysitter drove from Phoenix, and the people just kept coming. I was carried through the first week by the sheer force of their collective energy.

Amid the shock and sadness were glimmers of mirth. As we began to plan the funeral, my older sister had the situation well in hand. She'd always been a consummate organizer and problem solver, though her grand and generous solutions often took her husband by surprise. At one point, we discussed beverages for the post-funeral reception and she noted that quite a bit of beer and soda would need to be chilled.

"Don't buy her a refrigerator, please," my brother-in-law quipped.

The evening after the funeral, gathered in our family room, friends, nieces, and nephews began to tell funny stories about texts Roy had sent them. Unbeknownst to me, when I was reading myself to sleep every night, Roy was scrolling through Yahoo! and MSN on his phone, texting funny stories and pertinent articles to most of our family members. After several people shared such stories, my sister said, "Everybody in the room who received a text from Roy raise your hand." Nearly everyone did. It was funny and joyful and so characteristically Roy.

And then they all left.

I wanted this experience of support and camaraderie to last forever. Or at least for a few months. But of course, it couldn't. An abundance of love sustained me through the first week, but I didn't trust it to continue once everyone left. My tendency to compartmentalize experiences and label them good or bad led me to cling to the good. I only wanted safety, euphoria, joy, the connection of a miracle, or a supportive community to carry me along indefinitely. It also created in me a dependency on external influences to maintain my internal peace. I found comfort in reading about the disciples' wavering uncertainty after the miraculous feeding of a multitude.

The twelve men present for that miracle had decided at some point in their life to follow Jesus around wherever he went. Not just believe in him, but follow him around, listen to his talks, healings, and conversations, and see to his physical needs for food and rest. I imagined that as they continued to see how he operated in the world, their trust grew—and with it, their loyalty.

Christ's inconsistencies often bewildered his followers. After the disciples experienced the dramatic miracle of abundance and were riding high from it, they took a small boat out to cross the Sea of Galilee. They traveled on to their next destination, trusting that Jesus would follow. It got dark. The sea churned. Their boat tossed precariously in the waves. Fear spilled into the vessel.

They did the same thing I found myself doing when faced with yet another scary unknown: they looked outside themselves for the person they'd grown to trust. But he wasn't with them and hadn't followed. The disciples had just hours ago participated in a great mystery. They'd watched Jesus take two loaves of bread and five fish and feed five thousand people. It was a miracle of presence, abundance, and being. But did the miracle create constancy for the disciples? Did one miracle inspire them to trust in the next one? Not at all. As much as I wanted the constancy of my faith and trust to bring me placidly into the next moment, it rarely did. Instead, the disciples were in the boat and afraid. Again. Like me.

Love had sustained me so generously in my life. I saw many problems solved, fears relieved. But this time, I didn't know. Maybe this would be the time I'd be forsaken or abandoned. Roy's death bombarded me with insecurity—the paramedics, the doctors, the mystery, and the miracles had all failed him in his fight for life. But perhaps Roy wasn't fighting at all. Perhaps on some level he'd decided to go.

A lifesaving miracle might have provided the constancy I needed to sustain my faith. Instead, I found myself in a small boat in a raging sea. I longed for the constancy of the miracle, the answered prayer, the whisper of hope. Instead, I encountered the instability and insecurity of shock and loss.

The disciples probably experienced this longing too. When Jesus was present, they felt safe participating in the miracles flowing from a mysterious connection. When he stepped away, they began to feel the blowing wind and the stirring up of the sea. They feared he had abandoned them. What, instead, would create stability while experiencing the shifting elements? I realized that, like them, I looked to miracles for evidence to sustain my trust.

The story went on to say that after they had rowed out three or four miles, they saw Jesus coming toward them, walking on the water. The disciples' response? Fear. The story said, "And they were frightened."

How much did I allow fear to keep me from recognizing love? I had before me an invitation to seek the constancy of love within the mystery and uncertainty of death. However, unlike the child searching for the constancy of the caregiver who eventually appears, I had to trust myself even when no one walked on the water toward me, making me feel even a touch safer in my churning sea.

Scientists I'd read coaxed me into accepting that I lived in an uncertain universe. Growth, by its very nature, required change. While I couldn't pretend to grasp physicist Werner Heisenberg's uncertainty principle, the little I did understand inspired me to ponder how the material world of atoms, cells, elements, and human constructs was unstable and uncertain. Life presented this reality to me daily.

And yet I resisted.

As the disciples commenced to worrying again, Jesus tried to show them the truth of uncertainty. He seemed to imply that just because it had worked last time didn't mean it would work again. I imagined he was pushing them to see the constancy within the mystery—a constancy present in the mysterious, dark, still, and quiet space from which all energy emanates and to which all energy returns. For if, as physicists tell us, energy can be neither created nor destroyed, it must always exist somewhere, in some form.

Whenever I was confronted with something fearful and unstable, I'd think, I know this is it. This is not going to work out. This time, everything holding me up will come crashing down.

Once the disciples recognized it was Jesus, the story tells us, "They were willing therefore to receive him into the boat; and immediately the boat was at the land to which they were going."

In an instant, the disciples arrived at their destination—I almost missed that last little mystery, tucked into the story in its own quiet sentence. Once they let him into the boat, they arrived. First, Jesus defied the physical elements by walking on water. Then he defied the space-time continuum by taking a boat full of people instantly to their destination. The mysteries of healing were two-fold: circumstances could not only defy our physical understanding of the world, but also our understanding of space and time.

This often happened when Jesus was around.

Did he walk on water and mysteriously transport the boat out of necessity? Or did he do these little miracles to confound the disciples—to give them yet another experience of something beyond their understanding? I wanted my grief experience to be within my realm of understanding so badly that, as a result, I'm sure I missed much.

I imagined myself in the boat with those men, napping as the rest of the crew shouted that Jesus was coming toward them, walking on the water. I'd laugh and say, "You guys really are crazy." Then I'd go back to sleep. I'd wake up when the boat landed in Capernaum, stretch, and say, "Wow, I must have really slept. Felt like such a quick trip."

But Jesus kept pushing them, and me, beyond the signs. After the disciples let him into the boat, he said, "You seek me, not because you saw signs, but because you ate of the loaves and were filled. Do not work for the food which perishes, but for the food which endures to eternal life, which the Son of Man shall give to you."

I'd always enjoyed the thrill of synchronicity. Miracles amazed me. I loved them. There was a sort of high with them, perhaps like the disciples experienced after the five thousand were fed. When little miracles did occur, we liked to say it was such a *God* thing ... the cancer was cured, the money arrived, the fire stopped inches from the house. God was with me, I could tell by the signs. Like when Kendra showed up fresh from the University of Minnesota.

But signs, Jesus said, were not true constancy. The source of well-being was simply being with the truth of what is present. Letting go of the need for synchronistic events to create my foundation. Being with the uncertainty, and trusting. Being with the mystery, and questioning. Being with the pain, and finding comfort. It was not at all the linear process of suffering, healing, suffering, healing I hoped for. There was no future time and place where it was all going to come together in sweet resolution.

The first model of spiritual healing I constructed as a young adult suggested this linear process, with a defined beginning (diagnosis) and end point (healing). Suffering and pain led to awakening, which led to healing, which resulted in a life of peaceful unity with the creator. This model relied on material constancy.

The possibility of "happily ever after" dimmed through my experience with chronic illness. Spiritual disillusionment during my forties led me to revise the linear model into a sort of upward spiral. In this model, a catalyst of suffering disrupted my constructed beliefs; life didn't work out as I'd hoped. My resulting and sometimes desperate spiritual inquiry deepened the connection to my creator, helping me accept the suffering and open more to God. This circle then spiraled upward into a new consciousness.

I lived with this view of healing as I struggled with chronic illness for a long time. But Roy's death forced another revision, a more unitive—rather than linear or circular—way of understanding suffering and spiritual healing. My experience of pain, suffering, healing, and connection seemed to occur outside of time, all at the same time. I could no longer chart a tidy map for suffering, then healing. They existed together.

Like the funeral. It was so incongruent, the joy of having friends and family around as the shock of loss crept into my awareness. It felt irreverent to fall into the old joking, wisecracking banter of lifelong friends. But we did it. As we planned the ceremony, my sister told us of a service she'd recently attended that included humorous stories about a deeply loved man. So, we decided to add a bit of humor to Roy's service.

On the day of the funeral, as the prelude music faded out, my dear friend stepped to the podium and announced that we would open with one of Roy's favorite songs. The sound system came on with an old folk song Roy used to teach the kids, the Johnny Rebeck song. If you don't know it, it starts with, "Once there was a fat man, his name was Johnny Rebeck." My daughter put her arm around me as our friends and family sang along, uncertain what their reaction should be in this strange departure from tradition. Those behind me in the pews certainly didn't know whether my shoulders shook with laughter or grief. I knew it was both.

In the following days and weeks, I found myself stumbling into suffering at unexpected moments, but also stumbling into joy. And both at the same moment. When I recalled a particularly tender moment between Roy and me, I felt deep comfort and excruciating sorrow.

As my son and I walked the pilgrimage in Spain known as the Camino de Santiago, a journey we took to scatter Roy's ashes, he was always well ahead of me. But one day he stopped and waited for me at the crest of a hill. I looked up to see him standing sideways, the sun shining behind him, and for an instant I thought he was Roy, so familiar was the tilt of his hat, the hand on his walking stick, the drape of his clothing. A flash of memory moved through me: Roy and me navigating a Colorado river, fly rods in hand. In a single instant, I felt anguish for my loss and pride and joy in seeing so much of Roy's spirit reflected in our son.

What if the experiences I defined as separate, linear, and process-oriented were really a collective experience of being? Was it the nature of existence to defy resolution? The paradox was the constancy found within the mystery. Healing was found within the suffering in the ongoing flow of life. The flow, the river, the water. God. It was welcoming myself in the place I found myself.

THE EXPOSURE

ON THE MORNING ROY DIED, we'd had an argument. It wasn't a silly little argument; it was *the* argument. The one we'd been having throughout our marriage. The one that was really about unmet needs and unforgiven resentments. We'd been working on it in therapy, but in the rush and stress of an upcoming busy day, we succumbed to old habits. I had to take a conference call and we agreed to a temporary truce.

When I finished my call and went looking for him, I found him on the bathroom floor, agonal breathing the only respiration left to subside. A few weeks later, I lamented to my therapist: we were just playing our game. I didn't realize it was just our petty little game. Until I saw him lying there and realized the game was no more.

I was so ashamed about the argument that I waited six months before I talked about it in my grief group. Maybe I even believed our argument caused his death. And judged myself culpable. When I first brought it up in the group, their response surprised me. My fellow survivors clearly felt and empathized with my pain. Many looked my way with a knowing smile.

People argued. Especially married people. Yes, it was heart-wrenchingly open ended. We didn't get to apologies and forgiveness. We didn't get to a resolution. We didn't even get to say goodbye. But once I brought it into the group, shed some light into the dark little drawer where I'd stored it away, I learned that it wasn't a burden I had to carry.

Shame, an insidious little beast, had reared its ugly head with a vengeance. The experience of shame was not new to me; my thinly concealed unworthiness was perhaps the strongest force keeping me from spiritual healing. Lurking behind the flimsy wall of self-confidence was a looming shadow, diminishing me—the shadow imposed upon me and accepted by me in a million little moments of shame. This shame led me to what I considered the most poignant story in scripture, where Jesus approached a woman living deep in a place of unworthiness.

At the time of Christ's life, women were property and adultery was punishable by stoning the woman. The man wasn't held accountable. One day, while Jesus taught in the temple, a group of Pharisees drew attention to a woman who had been caught in the act of adultery. Their law commanded them to stone her, they explained, and they asked Jesus what he thought about it. The Pharisees clearly had at least two items on their agenda: to punish the woman by stoning her, and to test Jesus's knowledge of and acquiescence to their religious laws.

Most of us aren't challenged to publicly expose our needs, failures to conform to cultural standards, or hidden fears. But some of us are. And when we are, the highest spiritual purpose for this type of exposure is always an invitation to compassion.

In this story, Jesus began by taking his time. He stooped down and wrote with his finger in the dust. We aren't told what he wrote; I imagined him simply taking a pause, formulating how he would respond. Then he straightened up and skipped the theological discussion altogether. He addressed the spiritual issue with a single sentence: "He who is without sin among you, let him be the first to throw a stone at her."

The woman was exposed, he seemed to acknowledge, and you freely judged and condemned her. Now, which one of you would like me to expose your vulnerabilities in the same way?

Go ahead. Throw your stones. Then you'll be next. We don't need to have a theological conversation here about what your law says. Truth is truth.

The religious leaders left and Jesus stayed with the woman. He didn't condemn her; instead, he encouraged her to try to do a little better. He actually said, "Go and sin no more." What I heard in those words was Jesus gently saying, It's okay. It will go more easily for you if you just try and do a little better.

When others chose to shame the woman to death, Jesus touched her with forgiveness, compassion, and grace. In a single sentence—"Who among you will cast the first stone"—he pointed to my very human, knee-jerk temptation to cast people as "other" and judge and condemn.

What I hadn't seen before, however, was how much I also did this to myself.

As I struggled with the shame of my behavior on the morning Roy died, I discovered I didn't have to be afraid to look. The bond of suffering I shared with my grief group allowed me to bring dignity to my process. Their acceptance invited me to let go of self-judgment and condemnation. Hiding that piece of my story took a great deal of energy. It was a tricky business, the process of peeling away the scrim to expose the true story playing out behind it—whether a single incident, like my experience with Roy, or an imprint created over time. Bringing compassion to the shame and arriving at forgiveness took courage. Thank God for the compassion of grief groups. Thank God for the confidentiality of therapists.

Hidden parts of me, deep in the nooks and crannies of my psyche, seemed to collect shame like stalactites growing longer and longer as the moisture dripped down and clung to the bottom. Eventually, what was really nothing more than human nature grew so shameful to me that I couldn't expose it to anyone, let alone myself.

Shame wanted me to be an outcast. I felt it that day when I sat in grief group, anticipating rejection and judgment for my behavior—for arguing with Roy. Shame made me find ways to hide. It wanted me to forget about the argument, pretend to the world that it hadn't happened. But I would always know it had. My old shame-producing behaviors came with my constructed-self.

They weren't the true me. Beliefs growing in dark places didn't get released into the universe; rather, they stuck around to block the sun. Hidden toxic emotions bore down into my cells and ate away at my energy.

In *Daring Greatly*, Brené Brown talks about a study conducted by professor James Pennebaker and his colleagues at the University of Texas. They looked at what happened when rape and incest survivors kept their experiences secret compared to sharing their stories. Brown writes, "The research team found that the act of not discussing a traumatic event or confiding it to another person could be more damaging than the actual event. Conversely, when people shared their stories and experiences, their physical health improved, their doctor's visits decreased, and they showed significant decreases in their stress hormones."

In hiding what I didn't want to see about myself, I also hid from the Love observing those truths without condemnation. But awareness, forgiveness, and grace became new practices. In them, I saw the possibility of a unitive experience. The more I was fully present with all parts of myself, the less energy I spent hiding.

Reading about scientists' correlations between the spiritual and physical made me wonder if Christ knew about this energetic connection. He clearly demonstrated the sanctity of private confession and the resulting freedom from toxic, belaboring emotions in his brief encounter with the shamed woman.

The same consciousness that Christ brought to the wedding at Cana, when he protected the dignity of the host, appeared again in his interaction with the woman. He brought a quiet gentleness to a moment of exposure that had initially struck terror and shame into her heart—and into my heart when I anticipated exposure.

My therapist once addressed my tendency to hide from thoughts and behaviors I considered shameful. He asked if I had any dirty little secrets about my relationship with Roy.

"I'm not sure what you mean," I shot back.

"Just think about it," he said.

For the next week, I thought of little else. I guess I should thank my therapist for that little phrase: just think about it. He planted an idea and then let me spend the week ruminating. And the dirty little secrets showed up everywhere. Things I blamed Roy for. Things I chose to be angry about. The ways I often talked about him when he wasn't in the room. The little offenses I allowed to grow and fester. Hurtful teasing. Expecting him to provide the empowerment I wasn't feeling. And there they were again, on the day Roy died, fueling our final argument.

My leaning into self-awareness, a vulnerable process, was best done privately—exposure would have rallied my cavalry of defenses. And riding on the coattails of those defenses came toxic behaviors like judgment, condemnation, shame ... and hiding. Exposure also carried the potential for further wounding. As the story of the woman illustrated, deeply personal information put in the wrong hands could deepen the wound. The purpose of my exposure was not shame, but self-awareness and forgiveness. As I experienced both extending and receiving forgiveness, my belief that I was worthy of it grew, along with my ability to forgive myself.

The woman caught in adultery was publicly exposed and shamed as part of a political, theological, and intellectual challenge. The religious leaders wanted to engage Jesus in a legal discussion. I wondered how she felt. I was angry just imagining her exposure before those men, not only for condemnation but also to be stoned for the sake of their misogynistic politics. All while her male partner suffered no consequences whatsoever.

Was she frightened? Alone? Enraged? Did she weep? Did her body tremble as she listened to the men callously discuss her impending death? What was her experience of "self-knowing"? And what of the other women present, if any were there? One of the most heartbreaking experiences is to see women judge and shame other women.

A few years before Roy died, as I was tiptoeing into this life of self-awareness, my therapist led me on a meditation into my heart space. He asked me to describe what I saw there. The image, as vivid as if it were right next to me, was a small, wounded animal in the wild. A badger. Curled into itself, coat mangy, teeth bared, it snarled at anyone who dared to look in, let alone draw close. Powerfully, vulnerably exposed.

Fortunately, I was in the safe hands of an experienced, compassionate professional who showed me a gentle and courageous way to approach my shamed and wounded heart. Together, we forged a bridge of forgiveness and compassion.

Poet David Whyte invited me to this perspective in "Self Knowledge," an essay in *Consolations: The Solace, Nourishment and Underlying Meaning of Everyday Words.* He wrote, "Self-knowledge is often confused with transparency, but knowledge of the self always becomes the understanding of the self as a confluence; a flowing meeting of elements, including all the other innumerable selves in the world, not a set commodity to be unearthed and knocked into shape. Self-knowledge is not clarity or transparency or knowing how everything works, self-knowledge is a fiercely attentive form of humility and thankfulness."

And I would add worthiness. In her encounter with Jesus, the shamed woman experienced a connection. She was worthy. Worthy of the attention of Christ. Worthy of the justice he offered her. He directed his comments to the Pharisees, but the message to her came through. You are not alone. You are not less than these people condemning you. You are more than a pawn in their political game.

Whenever I anticipated exposure, I didn't trust myself with the naked truth about my choices, mistakes, and failures. I wasn't confident about moving into a new layer of grief. What a disappointment to find out that I wasn't who I wanted to be, who I thought I was, who I wanted others to think I was.

Brené Brown says worthiness is about belonging (which she defines as the innate human desire to be part of something larger than us). When I thought I needed to be perfect or live up to someone's expectations in order to belong, my inner shame told me how far I was from perfect and, therefore, how unworthy I was. But when instead, like the adulterous woman, I was introduced gently to the truth of my worthiness, imperfections and all, shame held less power for me.

The resulting spiritual practice felt like a Möbius strip, with two paths in perpetual flow. I brought a little light to my shame and, at the same time, I loved the desperate little self who'd created her way of survival. I practiced forgiving myself. I tried to do a little better. There was no period of resolution where my darker aspects were fully uncovered and accepted. It required living in a constant state of grace—a state of humility that cultivated compassion. And with compassion comes kindness. And with kindness toward the self comes inherent empathy toward others.

I saw that I could, at any given time, embody any of the characters in the woman's story. It became a bellwether for me: was I in the judging, shaming, finger-pointing crowd? Was I the shamed woman, exposed and vulnerable? Was I the ruling authority, making life decisions for other people based on what my ego needed? Yes. I could be any or even all of those people. I could also pause, stoop down, and write in the sand, reminding myself that the judging part of me was also the accused part of me. I was worthy of acceptance. I could be the forgiving one. And the forgiven one.

As I gently inquired into the shame that my argument with Roy caused, I used a few tools to come ever closer to resolution. When I sat in meditation and gingerly touched the aching wound of shame clamping down on my nervous system, I called up a healing memory. One in particular worked especially well for me.

Once, after a different argument, I left the house to walk it off around the lake in our neighborhood. As I ascended a small hill near home, I saw Roy walking toward me. As the distance between us slowly closed, he approached me with his characteristic silence. I looked at him, he looked at me. Then he took my hand and we walked the rest of the way home together. In times when I grieved the lack of resolution in our final argument, evoking this memory settled my nervous system and reminded me of our connection.

Most consoling to me was this truth: a single, untimely argument did not define our relationship. Our marriage was so much more. As time and attention healed the shock, memories showed up regularly with a range of emotional impacts. I couldn't eulogize a relationship rife with conflict and challenges; neither could I invoke shame about the consequences of our behavior. Instead, I chose to see our relationship as a beautiful tapestry woven with both darkness and light. We'd built a life together with a wide, passionate range of emotions—fierce anger, deep love, sweet humor, gentle forgiveness.

I once heard someone say that the loss of a loved one is a giant hole we fall into. As we negotiate a new reality, we climb out and fall back in regularly. Then we climb out and learn to navigate around it as the terrain around the hole grows, shrinking the hole's relative size. Then we simply step over it as we live in the new, expanded space.

I had to let shame intermingle with grief, find myself worthy of climbing out of it, and let my consciousness expand into something larger. Our marriage was so much more than a single argument. I was so much more than my transgressions.

THE BLAME

IT WAS A WARM SPRING DAY when everything wanted a peek at the sun: plants, animals, people. My student Henry and I were squatting together on the playground, watching a ladybug make its way across a span of concrete. The littles (that's what I called my toddlers), living so close to the earth, often spotted things we adults failed to see. Henry reverently kept his hands resting on his knees.

"Look," I said, relishing the teaching moment, "she's using her tiny little legs to crawl across the cement."

"Why?" he asked, his eyes intensely focused on the creature.

"Well, I suppose she needs to go somewhere."

"Why?" he asked.

I hadn't sensed the trap; I should've known better. I taught toddlers!

"Maybe she's looking for food."

"Why?" he asked.

We both looked up, heads nearly bumping, eyes locking. He gave me his big two-year-old grin. My first thought was, is this kid messing with me?

With young children, the first couple of times they'd ask why were usually motivated by sincere curiosity. I often thought I could actually see their little minds clicking away, pondering an explanation. But after one or two questions? I was pretty sure it was something else. A game, maybe. Or a desire to continue the attachment created by the conversation.

These conversations eventually lead to making up a response. It goes something like this:

"She's looking for food because she's hungry."

"Why is she hungry?"

"Because she was naughty, and her mother sent her to bed last night without her dinner."

No, no, no, that would never do.

Scientists call this speculation a theory. Storytellers call it a plot. Philosophers call it reason. "Why" has its useful place in the creative discourse of learning and discovery. And for those who suffer, "why" is one of the most compelling questions.

Unfortunately, when it came to healing my spiritual wounds, it fell short. I spent many grieving days on my mother's sofa repeating the phrase, "I just don't know what to do."

She sat next to me, shaking her head and saying, "I just don't understand why this had to happen."

It made me angry. My mother was over eighty years old and had lived a great deal of life. Didn't she have more to offer?

It wasn't her fault. I knew Roy's death didn't make sense. But I was frustrated when I couldn't resolve the depths of my misery with inquiry. In my human need to give reason to my suffering, I was left holding an empty bag. This led me on a very short trip from the angst of "why" to the smug satisfaction of blame. To ask why was a sincere seeking. Using it to place blame was a dead end.

Why did Roy die?

Because he couldn't get enough oxygen to his heart.

Why couldn't he get enough oxygen to his heart?

You see how this would go nowhere.

I have yet to meet someone who says, "You know, once I understood why that tragedy happened, I found healing and peace."

Jesus seemed to be trying to teach his disciples this truth when he healed a blind man they encountered on the road.

In this story, the disciples stepped right into the "why" game. They asked Jesus, "Rabbi, who sinned, this man or his parents, that he should be born blind?"

Jesus said, "It was neither that this man sinned, nor his parents; but it was in order that the works of God might be displayed in him."

My initial response was, My husband died so God might be displayed? Nazi Germany happened. Darfur happened. Mass shootings happened. This? So that God could be displayed? Thanks, but is there anything else on this menu?

And yet, as I found the courage to accept my own suffering, I also considered how suffering was as much a part of the human condition as breathing. I didn't ask why I breathed, why I lived, in the same way I asked, why do I suffer?

The question was pointless when I used it as a clever camouflage for blame. Blaming somehow distanced me from the pain, shifting it from the realm of emotion into the realm of intellect. To connect action and consequence was a natural result of my need to give reason to suffering.

I'd used it more subtly in the past. Blaming the parents when a child struggles with something: Oh, her poor daughter, in rehab again. Well, it's hard on the child when the mother travels all the time for work.

Or, oh, he has cancer. Well, he never did take care of himself.

But we all know people who took horrible care of themselves and lived to a ripe old age, and people who took terrific care of themselves and contracted terminal illnesses.

On yet a larger scale, I used blame to make sense of tragedy. If I could identify a culprit, the tragedy might make some sense: the terrorist, the disturbed adolescent, the deranged despot, the greenhouse gases. But what about tornados, earthquakes, tsunamis? What happened when I couldn't find anyone to blame? I could blame God as an omniscient, omnipresent being who pulled all the strings. Or I could question the existence of a God who didn't prevent suffering.

The link between God's judgment and tragedy was deeply embedded in my belief system. I could accept the possibility of God's hand in suffering endured by others, in a different place or time. But once suffering struck me, I was more inclined to work my way out of my belief in a punishing God. Yet I still felt unsettled about Divine presence in the face of suffering. Too frequently, I dismissed true anguish by settling on God's omniscient control. If God wasn't in this, I would think, then I can't make any sense of it. And I couldn't live in a world I couldn't make some sense of. I would go mad.

So, I created a God who allowed tragedy and suffering so I could be mad at something. This blame game gave suffering a reason, but it wasn't very satisfying.

I only created further suffering when the blame landed squarely on me, as it often did. Self-blame became a deserted island on which I landed, shipwrecked, with no hope of rescue. In my deep suffering, self-blame locked the energy of my experience in place. It allowed me to hold tightly to negative emotions rather than release them.

Self-blame was like picking at the scab of my wound. In the year before Roy's death, he put a tiny book by Thich Nhat Hanh, *How to Love*, in my Easter basket. I'd hoped we would read it together. When he died, I decided to embark on my own version of a Buddhist mourning ritual, honoring the forty-nine-day journey of spirit from this world to the next. Each day, I read a page in the tiny book and wrote a journal entry about the love we had missed. I can see how this ritual might sound like an excruciating and unnecessary journey into pain, but it helped me let go of the hopes I had for a growing, nurturing love as we moved into the next phase of our lives.

But each day, as Thich Nhat Hanh offered a loving practice, I blamed myself for not engaging in the practice more. This was the unnecessarily painful part of the exercise: blaming myself for not meeting my own expectations. Yet with it came a letting go. As I journaled letters to Roy and poured out my regrets, I let go of my self-expectations. And self-blame. It took time to give space to the regret contracting my heart. To feel gratitude for the relationship we had. To practice self-forgiveness for not achieving the relationship I had hoped for.

So, when I looked into Jesus's explanation in the story of the blind man, I got curious about the works of God. What I heard, in Christ's words, was that it wasn't about who sinned. It wasn't about blame. Finding cause and placing blame wouldn't heal the wound—suffering was about seeing the human propensity toward kindness and compassion in the face of great pain. The work of God. It was always about seeing God. It was the work of God in and among the suffering that brought healing.

In my grief-reading, one of the early and frequent messages was "welcome to the club nobody wants to be part of." It was true. Over the weeks and months, fellow club members began to show up at my home. A widow from my book group stopped by to drop off some books on grieving. Seeing my near catatonic state, she took extra time to gently coax me out of the house for a short walk around the neighborhood. A divorced friend I'd only recently met made a point to stop by on her way to a retreat, fixing me breakfast while I sat on the couch in my bathrobe, weeping. Another divorced friend lived with me for a month while in transition, filling my kitchen with the lovely aroma from her stovetop espresso machine, sharing stories of her own grieving experience on our regular walks.

God was there. And God could be found in the brotherhood or sisterhood among warriors, in the community of resistors during war, in the heroes carrying wounded citizens from a mass shooting. In the gentle touch of a doctor giving aid to a dying person. In the text from a friend, inviting a widow to get out of bed on another dark morning and walk into life. The Divine nature of humanity. A nature that never seemed to go away if I opened my eyes and heart to it.

I couldn't identify the exact moment when my mom's innocent "why" became an exercise in blame for me, but I found it to be a trap of the intellect. The intellect, trying to protect me from vulnerability, could spend hours, days, and years chewing over the question why, or searching for who or what to blame. Thinking long and hard about it created a distraction from the pain. But thinking didn't remove my suffering or heal my wounds.

I knew I wasn't alone in responding to the untimely, unexpected loss of a loved one by desperately seeking a reason. A reason, I thought, would help me make sense of the world again. Help me feel better. Why did my husband have a fatal heart attack? Was it something I did? Something his parents did? Even when it was someone's fault, the exercise was futile.

My intellect wouldn't get me where I wanted to be on the issue of suffering. What brought me there instead were the works of God—works of love. As I sat in pain and friends reached out to relieve my suffering with their compassionate presence, I experienced love. I experienced God in my connections with other human beings.

When my heart shattered, these touches of grace and mercy were magnified through the kaleidoscope of pain. I felt it in the compassion of the director at Roy's funeral; her sensitive approach to my suffering was not affected, but, as I learned later, the outcome of losing her own son. The day I had to pick up Roy's ashes, we met again. She held my hand and looked into my eyes deeply. "The light is beginning to return," she said.

I felt it in the unexpected boundaries others put on my suffering. I've seen the same Chinese medicine doctor for over twenty years. A few months after Roy died, I lay on the table, actually whimpering. She'd had enough. She gently rubbed my calf as she moved toward the door. "You're going to be fine," she said.

I felt like one of my toddlers who'd scraped a knee—in that split second when they looked at me to measure whether they should scream or dust themselves off, I'd usually smile and say, "You're going to be fine."

I felt it in the encouragements I received to return to activities I enjoyed. A friend invited me to ski for a couple of days, and I waffled. "Well, then, just bring your books," she suggested. "You can read and write and enjoy the mountains while we ski."

Once I was within reach of the slopes, I couldn't resist, as she'd probably guessed. But when we skied, I was horrified at my lack of stamina. I stopped frequently, and was only able to complete two full runs. My friend and her husband, both experienced with loss and grief, affirmed my victory at just getting back out there.

This new way of seeing the support and affirmation gently and quietly offered by others was the final lesson Christ brought to his encounter with the blind man. There was a bit of a double meaning to the story. It was about being physically blind and then seeing, but it was also about being blind to the love of God and opening one's heart to seeing and feeling new spiritual experiences. Jesus gave the suffering man, blind since birth, his sight so he could see the love of God manifest in his life. A physical resolution for a spiritual healing.

Suffering raised my defenses and created bitterness and anger. I initially responded with questions and blaming. But as friends and family responded to my suffering with love, my heart opened to spiritual experiences I might not have known otherwise. As I accepted the deep suffering in my life, my heart, over time, softened. I encountered new levels of vulnerability and opportunities for grace and mercy.

My daughter once prompted me with this question: "Agree or disagree. You can have suffering without love, but you can't have love without suffering."

I answered, "I believe you can have love without suffering, but not at its deepest and most profound level. Because suffering brings us to a vulnerable place where our defenses are down and we're most open to receiving."

Psychologist and contemplative James Finley summarized John of the Cross in his book *Intimacy: The Divine Ambush*, saying that we get all tangled up both in suffering and in searching for love.

"There is no such thing as deprivation of love," Finley writes, "but there is deprivation of the capacity to experience the love that is never missing. Therefore, my spiritual practice is to look within for the places that are blocking my ability to experience the flow of an immense tenderness that is endlessly giving itself to me in all situations."

No resolution here. No making sense of tragedy. No answers to our most heart-wrenching whys. Asking why, placing blame, Jesus seemed to be saying, wouldn't help.

THE DOORKEEPER

ON A BLEAK JANUARY DAY IN 2007, under an overcast Chicago sky, my father and I made small talk as we drove from the suburbs to Northwestern Memorial Hospital in the heart of the city. We both knew that the stem cell transplant he would begin when we arrived might extend his life. We also knew that it might kill him. But we didn't talk about it. I had no inclination to probe the landscape of his fears, the source of his courage. Instead, I let him ramble about old work experiences, friendships, whatever came to his mind.

When we arrived, I was escorted to a waiting area while he was admitted and ushered into the room where he'd spend the next thirty days as his stem cells were harvested and his immune system was destroyed.

To get to his room, I walked through a set of double doors that looked no different than those on any hospital ward I'd been in. But once through those doors, I found myself in a small enclosure with another set of doors opposite, which had no handles on my side. I heard a quiet whoosh as the air I brought in was suctioned out and replaced with sterile air. Or so I imagined. I waited. When the whooshing subsided, the double doors to the ward opened automatically. I was invited to scrub my hands and put on a sterile robe. I walked into the room and saw my larger-than-life father lying in his hospital bed, made completely susceptible to any random germ floating in his environment.

My father. The man who dressed in a suit and tie every morning and went to work engineering the installation of large-scale HVAC systems. My father, who I don't remember being sick very often. My father, who could fix any appliance, design and build additions onto our house and a cabin by himself, change the oil in my car and tend to his immaculately manicured yard. The man who kept our family running like a well-oiled machine. The man who made me feel safe, insisted on my independence, and made me feel special like no one else could.

My father, who was about to let go of every protective cell he had. I resisted the heart-contracting fear I felt in seeing him so vulnerable. He wasn't capable of fighting even a mild virus or bacteria. I reminded myself that he was sequestered in a hospital unit for heightened care and protection. I was comforted by the trappings of his sterile environment, sur-rounded by trained professionals committed to his healing. In this physically compromised and vulnerable state, his need for protection was apparent. There was little shame in it.

After Roy's death, as I experienced powerlessness, I reflected on my time in my father's hospital room. I wanted a spiritual equivalent to his ICU: a safe place where I could be protected while some part of me was dying completely with an unpre-dictable outcome. But no such ICU existed—I had to create my own in order to enter into the courageous work.

My ICU was an interior place where I gently approached aspects of my wounded humanity and opened my soul to con-nect with Love. When I opened myself spiritually, I felt not only shyness, but also a terrifying vulnerability. In my wound-edness, I instinctively sought to protect. As I learned through unfortunate small-group experiences, the risk in exposing my spirit in order to heal was that I would also be opened to more pain.

In *A Hidden Wholeness: The Journey Toward an Undivided Life*, author Parker Palmer says the soul is shy, like an animal in the wild. He writes, "If we want to see a wild animal, we know that the last thing we should do is go crashing through the woods, yelling for it to come out. But if we will walk quietly into the woods, sit patiently at the base of a tree, breathe with the earth, and fade into our surroundings, the wild creature we seek might put in an appearance. We may see it only briefly and only out of the corner of an eye—but the sight is a gift we will always treasure as an end in itself."

The soul imagined as a shy wild animal resonated with me. I was also reminded of Jesus's images of people as sheep. Not wild animals; gentle animals incapable of providing their own protection, needing the safekeeping of a shepherd. My soul was both: shy and wild. Gentle and strong. Needing a place of safety in order to be truly accessible.

Jesus told a story called the parable of the good shepherd. In it, he used images of sheep and shepherds because they were familiar to his listeners. He evoked the safety of the sheepfold, the pen shepherds kept their flocks in at night to safeguard them from danger. He called himself the "good shepherd" and compared the safety he offered to protection from the dangers of thieves, robbers, or hired shepherds who didn't know their sheep. He said, "I am the good shepherd, and I know my own, and my own know me."

After hearing this, the Jewish authorities attempted to stone Jesus. He was getting dangerously close to the edge that eventually led to his death. Traditional Christian interpretations cite this verse as Jesus's claim to divinity.

But I didn't focus on the story's theological issues in my healing. Instead, I focused on the image of the sheepfold. I imagined it as a place of spiritual safety that I entered and left as Christ's love stayed ever near, ever present, for me to experience. The sheepfold became for me a tender, quiet place where I examined my wounds, self-inflicted and otherwise, and tended to them. My spiritual ICU.

This was the courageous act Jesus referred to when he invited us to enter the door into the fold of the sheep, claiming his place as doorkeeper. I imagined him saying, Enter through love, into your interior place where the soul connects with the Divine.

It was courageous because when I entered that space, when I opened myself spiritually, vulnerability set off my fight-or-flight response like a car alarm.

I didn't find my spiritual ICU in the trappings of traditional sacred spaces such as sanctuaries, synagogues, or stupas. Instead, I accessed this place of safety and healing with my imagination. In the *His Dark Materials* trilogy by Philip Pullman, characters used a magic knife to slice into alternate fields of time and space. An opening to the alternate universe showed up like a window dangling in midair, and the characters who stepped through it found themselves transported. This image helped me visualize a similar opening to the spiritual world. I looked for a seam where the material and the spiritual melded, where I could step through a window or door and find myself opened to a more expansive understanding.

In the parable, Jesus described himself as the doorkeeper. "I am the door; if anyone enters through me, he shall be saved, and shall go in and out, and find pasture."

He seemed to be saying something about access. About moving into Divine Love through him. He was at the door, the portal to love, where the sheep safely went in and out. I accessed this portal through awareness, prayer, meditation, and imagination.

Imagination was a priceless tool in my spiritual healing. An essential part of the design of the human psyche, imagination helped me access Divine Love.

In their book *The Healing Imagination: The Meeting of Psyche and Soul*, Ann and Barry Ulanov say, "Things are constantly reborn in the imagination, made fresh, brought to us to renew themselves and to renew us." The imagination, they write, "expresses psychic life, which speaks first in images before it speaks in words."

As a bridge between psyche and soul, imagination is engaged through symbol, myth, story, and image. Reading this, I was struck by how patriarchal Christianity (among other influences) produced in me an imagination populated with punishment and meritocracy. Beliefs lurking in my conscious and unconscious mind connected safety and worthiness with obedience and conformity. I recalled moments of palpable fear as I studied biblical passages about an angry God waiting for me to screw up so he could punish me. These limiting beliefs had found a home in the collective unconscious through centuries of teachings and practice. They kept me fearful of a damning misstep. In the face of this, however, I had the delightful opportunity to use my imagination to fashion my world differently.

In grief, I used imagination to bring healing emotions to traumatic memories. One of my grief-reading books was Neale Donald Walsch's *Home With God: In a Life That Never Ends*. In it, he suggests that when people are about to die, the soul is given a choice to stay on earth or transition to heaven.

This was a strange and unsettling concept to me until one day when, in meditation, I visualized the day Roy died. I didn't intentionally evoke the images I encountered; they just seemed to flow into my awareness. In my visualization, as the paramedics worked on Roy's body, he and I sat on the couch discussing why he had to leave. We both wept as he explained to me his reasons for going and I told him I understood. We embraced, then held hands, looked into each other's eyes, and said our goodbyes. There was both a sense of permanence and a temporary nature to our letting go. Though I knew I wouldn't see him again in my lifetime, I had the very strong sense that we would encounter each other again.

It was an imaginal healing space. A space where I claimed the goodbye we were robbed of. A space of deep love, longing, and sadness. A space of tender compassion. Trauma had instilled in my nervous system the unsettling emotions of shock, terror, and anxiety produced by our abrupt disconnection that day. The imaginal space we inhabited together brought healing emotions to that same memory. I returned to it frequently.

When I entered my healing imaginal space, Love was both the doorkeeper and the guide. It was a sacred space. In the beginning, I desperately wanted an external guide; someone outside me who would magically produce healing. But I came to realize that no person could see and touch my wounds the way I could. My soul connecting to God spoke to my shy, frightened animal, inviting me to imagine a new way of responding to my circumstances.

My meditative imagining of Roy's leaving was one of my earliest encounters in this sacred space. It was a gift. But I didn't trust that I could go in and out of my imaginal space and use it as a healing experience at will. I needed encouragement from my therapist. Trusting the unknown was another risk. I had to find the medicine of spiritual healing in this experience in order to build the trust to return.

In the story of the good shepherd, Jesus saw the disciples. As individuals. It was quite an extraordinary, and intimate, thing to be seen. To be known by name. I imagined my innocent-self recognized, and the fragile beginning of trust grew.

I tiptoed toward trust, and Love affirmed itself by its availability. The sheepfold was always there—it was I who went in and out of this healing space. Limiting beliefs informed by fear could be replaced with tools of spiritual healing.

I practiced accessing God within me, my higher self, by experiencing what it felt like to be invited, accepted, and forgiven. I set aside time to be available to both myself and Love, listening and hearing. Private, comfortable space and uninterrupted time helped me release physical and spiritual tensions, providing an opening out into the pasture for silence, imaginal meditation, nurturance. Paying attention to my body helped me open to self-awareness. As I became familiar with this level of awareness, I felt safe to go more deeply into complex and difficult emotions.

I had to be educated in emotional fluency before I could move to emotional resilience. It took time for me to learn to feel my emotions, let them move through, and return to a balanced place.

Early on, my therapist would say to me, you're angry, enraged, terrified. I would often say to myself, oh, that's what that feels like!

In one session, I described my enthusiasm in watching a documentary about women helping underserved and third-world communities in really extraordinary ways.

He said, "They inspire you."

I stopped and thought, yeah—I guess I've never recognized feeling inspired before.

The imaginal space didn't always resolve or transform the emotion. Sometimes, I simply sat with it. I spent a lot of time reflecting about the morning Roy died, and the many other things I might have done besides what actually transpired. At the time, frozen in shock, I stood in the living room staring out the window while the EMTs worked on him in our bedroom. I watched from a distant place as they wheeled a gurney through the hallway, pumping air into his lungs with what looked like no more than a plastic bag. I didn't even watch as they put him in the ambulance and drove off to the hospital without me.

Later, I tumbled through questions. What if I'd been in the bedroom with him, urging him to stay with me? What if I'd been in the ambulance, talking to him and loving him? And I wondered and wondered whether any of those things would have saved his life. A futile exercise of the mind, but one rife with self-blame, remorse, and regret. I took these thoughts and emotions into the sheepfold to compassionately hold the shame, the feeling of being responsible for his life, the need and desire to be in control. I could accept and forgive myself. I'd done the best I could.

I found the image of the pasture and the doorkeeper calming. Images were one of the Divine's ways of getting my attention and helping me understand the spiritual experiences available to me. With Divine Love as the gatekeeper, I could come and go and find rest and healing in this safe space, as Jesus promised when he said, "Come to me, all who are weary and heavy-laden, and I will give you rest."

I listened to myself hash over thoughts. I felt the emotions the thoughts evoked. I encouraged the thoughts and feelings to fully express. I gently moved myself to a place of loving acceptance.

Early in this practice, the intensity of my emotions scared me. I couldn't have done it without my therapist's expert, compassionate help. As he guided me to do this, I learned to trust my own boundaries as I rode the waves of emotion. He kept me present when I wanted to flee into dissociation (as I often did). When I could be fully present with my experience and find the strength to feel the emotions, I felt more safety moving through it. I felt safe with myself in this sacred, healing space.

For me, being present with the intense emotions of grief required a pasture (sacred space) and a doorkeeper (love). Before I could do this for myself, my therapist stood in for the doorkeeper. He knew how desperately I needed to access the emotions, but also how exposed they made me feel. He helped me learn how to enter in and when to go out. For others, the stand-in doorkeeper might be a friend, confidant, or parent.

On a practical level, a fellow widow told me about setting the timer on grief. Her counselor encouraged her to set her kitchen timer for thirty minutes, go into the emotion and cry as much as she needed, but come out of it when the timer went off. She would exercise, cook a meal, or do laundry—whatever got her back on an even keel again.

Psychologists call this emotional resilience. To enter into an emotion but not let it take over; to feel it move through. In her memoir *My Stroke of Insight*, neuroscientist Jill Bolte Taylor says that the average duration of an emotional experience is only ninety seconds. Any longer and our thoughts feed the emotion like oxygen feeds a fire.

Even after all my hard work to understand and move through my emotions, I was still surprised when grocery stores triggered me. In the months after Roy's death, this anxiety soared to a level that caused me to avoid the grocery store altogether. It evoked memories of shopping together, of him gently rubbing my neck as we waited in the checkout line or whispering something funny in my ear about the guy slicing our deli meat. Even anticipating the grocery store made me panic.

It took almost a year, but eventually I did go. My daughter encouraged me to try it; I just picked up a few things. As I was standing in the checkout line, I started to feel the fluttering in my stomach and my thinking got scrambled. But I was able to notice the fight-or-flight response and say to myself, oh, here it is. Anxiety.

I breathed. Nobody around me noticed my quiet, calming breaths: in, one, two, three, four, out, one, two, three, four. I reminded myself to feel my feet on the ground. I walked to the counter, ran my credit card through the reader, and intentionally, slowly, walked to the exit. I willed myself not to run.

I did it.

By allowing the emotion to have its time, to "run through its lines," as I liked to say, the emotion began to subside. By acknowledging and allowing, I was able to embrace and breathe through it. No need to panic about panic. It was only temporary. And most importantly, I learned that I could not only survive, but I could also use the energy of emotion on behalf of my healing.

Each person has access to the gift of imagination to create their own sheepfold, their own pasture of safety, and to choose their guide. For me, the sheepfold had to include an enormous amount of physical and emotional space. In crisis, I needed help with the day-to-day things so I could be present with the intensity of emotion. My sheepfold included the beautiful collective consciousness of other people's stories in books, novels, podcasts, texts, and messages. I engaged in the quiet of meditation and the flow of writing. This safe sheepfold was a space I learned to cultivate for myself.

For this healing to work, I had to trust the doorkeeper. The portal into my connection with the Divine was Christ's consciousness, alive through the Holy Spirit. I came face-to-face with what or who I really trusted to guide me on the journey. I explored other guides: friends, spiritual leaders, writers, nature. But I always came back to Christ, to Love in human form.

Jesus, my doorkeeper, continued to expand in my awareness as I learned more about his life on earth, his teachings, his expression to me through the Holy Spirit—and also through the circumstances and the people in my life. This, I said to myself, was Christ-consciousness.

My dad lived through his traumatic stem-cell transplant. He gained ten years against the cancer ravaging his blood. He not only survived, but thrived because of the safe cocoon provided at his body's most vulnerable time. I felt the same way about the sacred, spiritual space I entered as I healed. Love met me in my crisis and provided an imaginal healing practice that included safety, gentleness, tenderness, compassion, rest, hope, peace, and joy.

THE HOUSE

FOR TWENTY YEARS, EVERY JULY, my family packed up the car and drove seven hours to Wilderness Ranch, in southern Colorado. We joined three other families for a week of hiking, fishing, horseback riding, and hanging out. The week was steeped in traditions like the first-morning pancake breakfast, burgers at Freeman's General Store, fish tacos at Kip's Grill, or hanging in Creede. We spent smoky nights by the fire making s'mores and playing "three truths and a lie." We followed our children from their toddler years through college, careers, weddings, and everything in between.

The trip out of the city and over mountain passes always invited me to relax. I'd knit in the passenger seat, letting Roy deal with the kids' needs and squabbles. I felt my energy revive as we gained elevation and the air around the car cooled, the sun playing tag through a landscape of pine trees. When I finally saw the Rio Grande from my window, I'd put my knitting aside and watch the afternoon light tickle the rushing water.

The highway would give way to a two-lane road, then gravel, and finally dirt as we ascended through a mosaic of evergreen and aspen. When we crested the final hill, I would watch for the sleepy seven-cabin camp nestled around a small lake. It looked like a postcard. Over those years, the imprint of star-filled nights, dusky-gray sunsets and tranquil mornings found a home in my soul.

And then it didn't. Even though we scattered some of Roy's ashes at the ranch with an intimate group of family and supporters, I only visited once after he died. I just didn't want to return. My kids didn't want to either. Everything felt different. It wasn't just Wilderness that felt like home to me; it was Wilderness with Roy. Without Roy, it held less comfort. As with most of my life. Over thirty-three years, Roy had become central to both my physical and spiritual home.

I imagined that Jesus had, in a similar way, become a home for his disciples. I often wondered about the twelve men who left their homes to literally and figuratively follow Christ. What had they chosen to leave behind? Friends, surely. Possibly families and sources of livelihood. Letting go of the familiar and comfortable, they chose to follow and love a radical. Jesus was their person just as Roy was my person. And they were about to lose him.

One of our friends from Wilderness lost her husband to cancer three years before Roy died. One day as we chatted, she said, "You know what I miss most?"

"What?" I asked.

"He got me."

Yep. No one else knew me with as much depth and breadth as my husband. I came home to him after my endless business trips, my random world adventures, my father's death. I came home to him when I was thrilled and when I was exhausted. I sought refuge in him as I panted my way through labor and wrote my way through grad school. He was the only person in my life with whom I could secretly have a cigarette and drink scotch and complain. Who knew and loved my artsy bohemian side.

I had to completely redefine what I called home. When Jesus anticipated a similar loss for his disciples, he also talked about home. He said, "Let not your heart be troubled; believe in God, believe also in me. In my Father's house are many dwelling places; if it were not so, I would have told you; for I go to prepare a place for you. And if I go and prepare a place for you, I will come again, and receive you to myself; that where I am, there you may be also. And you know the way where I am going."

In his final days, he knew the disciples didn't comprehend what was about to happen. He would leave them. They would find themselves alone, without direction or connection. He was trying to point them toward spiritual realities to draw on for sustenance as they slid into despair.

Archetypally, a house or dwelling represents a sacred space, a sanctuary, a place of safety and containment. Spiritually, it represents the seat of our soul. Christ wanted the disciples to know that a spiritual place existed for and within them—a place of safety and inclusion unique to each of them.

"There are many dwelling places," he told them.

And, especially, he wanted to assure them that he was going ahead of them to prepare their place. The place where they could connect to and live with the Divine.

I caught a glimpse of Jesus's meaning as my first grieving summer gave way to autumn. One day, relieved to have Kendra doing the driving, I arrived at my weekly acupuncture appointment. This practitioner had treated me throughout my healing journey, and she was especially important to me in those early months of grief. As I walked up the steps into the small bungalow housing her practice, I noted the leaves changing color. Just stepping through the door into the quiet space calmed me. I sat on the treatment table in the tiny room, legs swinging like a child's.

"How are you today?" she asked.

"Disconnected."

"Disconnected how?" she prodded, a hint of concern in her warm eyes.

"I don't know. Homeless?" I said. I was both exhausted from trying to find words to describe my experience and desperate for someone to understand.

"Ah," she responded. "You're calling your soul back in."

She smiled. Then she exercised her lovely and sometimes frustrating practice of silence, allowing me time to absorb her words.

I lay on the table, the autumn light spilling over the blanket covering me, and pondered. I hadn't known my soul was out. I mentally worked at it a bit. But hadn't I offered pieces of my soul to Roy, in loving him? The reality of our shared existence—the physical, energetic, and spiritual—hit me. I needed to call home the parts of my soul that had intermingled with his.

Around the same time, I encountered the first medical form requiring an emergency contact. I'd used the same emergency contact for thirty-three years. His phone number changed over time, but Roy would always be the one to answer. With a shaky hand, I filled in my daughter's name and number. It felt like a heavy burden to place on her.

I saw in Jesus's description of his father's house not so much a physical home, but an experience of transformation: a new spiritual home. Jesus wasn't describing a place called heaven where the disciples would land after they died. Instead, he spoke of a spiritual reality that was accessible at any time. Just like when I emerged from the spiritual ICU and was invited into a healing transformation. A new spiritual place to dwell.

In one of his daily meditations, Richard Rohr talked about how the three stages of spiritual development happen in a linear fashion: from order, to disorder, to reorder. My reorder had been, as my acupuncturist described, a calling in of my soul. I called it "returning to self." Not the constructed-self of my ego, but my true self, now able to allow darkness and light to coexist, to accept the paradox.

In the same meditation, Rohr wrote, "Once we can learn to live in this third spacious place, neither fighting nor fleeing reality but holding the creative tension, we are in the spacious place of grace out of which all newness comes. God is now in charge, not us."

In learning to recognize paradox and mystery, I felt safe enough to open to a loving consciousness who knew me more deeply than I knew myself—and continued to reveal more of who I was. Who I was as a child, a woman, a college student, a wife, a mother, a professional, a writer, an artist.

A widow.

This unfolding was the spiritual stuff of life. To be at one with God was to live in the place where I found a safe, life-giving energy in perpetual renewal. A place of openness, curiosity, and stillness. It could be about imagination and trying and failing and creating. About stepping into the wonder of possibility.

When my son and I hiked the Camino, I was a bit cautious about the adventure. As the movie *The Way* showed, the true pilgrimage experience required waking each day and setting out on the journey with only a vague idea of where you'd be at the end of the day. Sleeping arrangements, while easily accessed and plentiful, were left to chance. Not quite ready for the true pilgrimage experience, I worked with a professional tour group who crafted a route complete with a private room and bath at the end of each day.

Even with those assurances, I still woke each morning with the feeling that I was venturing into the unknown. I had my guidebook with a rough map. I had a directory with the location of my next hotel, along with directions for how to find it when I reached the village. My son took a picture of the daily information page and took off. With a bit of guidance from hotel staff, each day I found the yellow arrow leading to the path and walked until I saw the next yellow arrow. I kept following the yellow arrows or the scallop-shell symbols until, tired and thirsty, exhilarated by the journey but thankful to be home for the day, I stumbled into the next village.

I had delightful experiences along the way. I met people, walked with them awhile, and walked on. I stopped at hermitages and cathedrals. I ate with strangers and by myself. I felt the warm sun on my face and the cold wind blow through my hair. And when, after the trip, I sorted through my photographs, I thought, what a great way to live each and every day. To wake in the morning with a vague idea of where I wanted to be at the end of the day. And then to just follow the signs.

Living a life connected with Love could be far more than a prescription for heavy spiritual challenges. It could also be an invitation to hold intentions loosely, to listen to promptings and nudges, to make new friends, to follow the signs, to be open to detours into the unexpected and unknown.

I first attempted to enter this space of connection through meditation. My meditation practice began long before I lost Roy. At the time, I'd grown weary of prayer groups where we spent an hour sharing prayer requests and ten minutes with eyes closed and heads bowed, reciting a laundry list of anxieties to God. I wanted something different from prayer, but I didn't yet know what it was.

I learned about a practice called contemplative prayer and found a group in my town who practiced regularly. I was thrilled to find, on my first visit, people who didn't share prayer requests. Instead, they sat down, did a short reading, and gently tapped a singing bowl. Soft vibrations settled over the space, and then … silence. For twenty to thirty minutes. Together. I was astounded. I continued to explore and practice the methods pioneered by Father Thomas Keating, Cynthia Bourgeault, and Richard Rohr.

At home, I could sit still for five minutes. But my group was so encouraging.

"Great!" they said when I told them. "Five minutes is great! Look at the progress you're making."

Over many years, I expanded my time in silent meditation. I've experienced soul-filling connection. I've also experienced, more often, restless agitation and the need to return to my intention by silently calling up a sacred word, chosen by me for this purpose. I learned to continually return to my sacred word when my mind acted like a child in a bouncy house, thoughts and ideas popping in and jumping up and down on the silence.

Gradually, I opened into a more constant and spacious place within myself. My sheepfold had become safer and more familiar as I gently explored stillness. I watched thoughts and emotions arise and miraculously move through, returning to stillness. I slowly constructed my new home.

It felt similar to the process I learned in a watercolor class I decided to attend, following the recommendations to try out new experiences as a remedy to grief. A friend invited me to a class with a very special teacher. I purchased little tubes of paints and expensive paper and brushes and approached the class with all the left-brained administrative skills that had served me so well in the business world.

"Ah," people would respond when I told them about my new hobby. "You've picked the toughest kind of painting to do."

How hard could it be? I thought.

Our teacher started mercifully slowly, demonstrating the beauty of colors flowing together across a sheet of paper that she deftly moved and coaxed into something lovely. I didn't get it. When it was time for me to sit at my own little table with a tub of water and a paint palette, I took out my pencil and carefully drew a grid of two-inch boxes on my paper. None of this weird and uncontrollable flow for me. I was only willing to explore contained spaces where I controlled how I put paint on the paper and how I mixed the colors and where the paint flowed. I finished with a nice sample grid of blues.

As she strolled around the room watching us, the teacher paused at my work. "Nice," was all she said. I sensed I'd missed something. At the next lesson, she continued to encourage those of us who really wanted to control the paint on the paper to let go and allow the paint and water to mix and flow as it desired.

"Risky, right?" she said with a twinkle in her eye.

She showed us how to draw shapes lightly with pencil, brush water into the shapes, and then drop in some color; how the paint followed its own way but stayed within the edges of the pencil lines. I became fascinated. In the following lesson, she showed us how to load a large brush with paint and sweep it in broad gestures across the paper.

Watercolor was a difficult medium because controlling the paint rarely got the desired effect. Watercolor work was beautiful primarily because of the free flow of water and paint as colors mixed in unexpected ways, producing lovely surprises. I slowly caught on to the experience of creating the intention of my painting with light pencil lines—more the impression of a bouquet than the details. I stepped into not really knowing what was going to happen on the paper; I began simply engaging in and enjoying the process. I produced lots of weird, undefined images. And a few lovely gems.

I found the courage to put my rigid grid of colors in its place: as a disciplined study of color mixing. The magic showed up as I practiced letting go, into the flow of paint and water, into dropping my expectations and stepping into the unknown with nothing more to protect and guide me than a loosely drawn intention.

The stillness I found in meditation ebbed and flowed through my daily life like water and paint mixing on paper. I used the grids in my life to keep the administrative details clicking along, but, as with my travels on the Camino, the unplanned was necessary for my pilgrimage into an experience. Like the surprising gems that arose when the paints ran into their own unexpected beauty.

Courage invited me to step into the wonder of possibility. To enter the place where Christ was, his father's house. Not an afterlife in a make-believe-heaven, but a spiritual place of expansive stillness where all possibilities originate. He said he went to prepare a place for the disciples. He promised to come again and receive them to himself.

"That where I am, there you may be also."

Maybe the new place I called home wasn't as elusive as I thought. Maybe it was in me and I was in it. Always. He also said, "You know the way where I am going."

It was a freeing idea, one that transcended my desire to find a safe home in rigid traditions. He promised: I knew the way.

THE VINE

THE DAY ROY DIED, TIME SLOWED AND THICKENED. A police officer drove me to the hospital and escorted me to the reception desk, where a kind woman asked me to sit in the waiting room.

Sitting there, I had a memory from just a few months back, of waiting in the same room for something benign and hearing the wail of a grieving woman behind a flimsy makeshift wall. I was horrified. She must have received tragic news, protected from the eyes around her but not the listening ears. I had watched discreetly as a young woman in a sweatshirt and leggings was escorted out by an older woman. Her tribe of family and friends followed behind, shock and disbelief carried in their solemn movements.

Coming out of that memory, I slowly returned to the present as I saw a middle-aged woman in street clothes coming my way. Not a nurse, I realized instantly. A social worker.

Before she could get too close, I spoke loudly across a row of seats. "He's gone, isn't he?"

"I can't tell you that," she said quietly, gently approaching. "The doctor would like to speak with you if you would just come with me."

And I knew then, because she was ever so slowly coaxing me to that makeshift room.

Before I'd left for the hospital, I had called our therapist and left a message. At some point, he joined me in the awful little room, though I barely noticed him. Until a young man in green scrubs came in, sat down, and gently told me that Roy had died nearly instantly of a heart attack.

I interrupted his calm explanation with a primal wail, launching myself from my chair. I collapsed into the arms of our therapist. I felt him brace to catch the unexpected impact, then anchor himself to the earth and find strength to hold me fast.

Time stood still. Until I recounted the events later, I had no idea how much time passed from the moment I first found Roy until I returned home with my son, carrying the Ziploc bag with Roy's wallet, some change, two dollar bills, and a receipt he'd had in his jeans pocket. By then, I'd contracted so deeply within myself that I needed a great deal of time before I could begin reentering the world. The world that was still marking time in neatly organized segments called minutes, hours, days.

At first, I counted in hours. The following day, I consciously marked the hour of his death and noted, with a clutching in my gut, that he'd been gone for twenty-four hours. Then, I counted in weeks. On the fourth Friday, I had a sense of time slipping away. If I could stay in a timeless space, Roy wouldn't be gone. Acknowledging the passage of time was my first tentative move out of shock.

It took me well over a year to expand out of myself enough to fully connect with my children's suffering. I wasn't ignoring it; I listened to them, read their words, saw their tears. I simply had no space within myself to absorb their experience. My grief was a solo affair, excruciatingly self-centered. My daughter said she only really began to process her own grief after a year because she'd been so concerned about my well-being. Our therapist told me that my kids feared losing not only their father, but also their mother. The pain of trauma so contracted my heart that I couldn't see beyond the cloud of my own suffering.

Time standing still. Perhaps anticipating when his friends, the disciples, would also have this contracting experience, Jesus shared with them another parable, a story about vines and branches. He said, "I am the vine, you are the branches; he who abides in me, and I in him, he bears much fruit; for apart from me you can do nothing."

My wounds opened me to a tenderness in this parable. I was, again, curious about their relationships. Thirteen men traveling together, living together, eating together. Twelve of these men seeing occurrences they never thought possible: people healed, cared for, even brought back to life. What did they talk about? Did they discuss their own troubles? Their beliefs and philosophies? We aren't privy to their general conversations. Only to a few brief interactions.

I imagined them to be connected in a deep, meaningful way. I was sorry the scriptures didn't give us more information about the scenes and settings of Jesus's conversations with his friends. But they did allow me to imagine. When he decided to tell them about the vine and branches, had they, perhaps, just eaten a meal of fish roasted over a fire? Were they dusty and tired from a day of traveling? Or chilled and damp, the salt of the sea under their nails? I saw them in a circle, close in around a fire to better hear Jesus as he quietly entreated them to continue the work they'd begun together.

He acknowledged the strength of their connectedness as friends. He anticipated their sorrow and disorientation after his death, their deep contraction as a possible reaction. As he shared this parable with them, he expressed his profound love for them. A love they could also share with one another.

In this parable, I saw Christ daring to hope that they would get beyond their contracted suffering and revisit their shared radical vision for the world. He called himself the vine and his disciples the branches. God, he said, was the vinedresser.

He asked them to continue to grow in him and promised he would grow in them as well. At first, the mutuality sounded weird to me. How could beings grow within one another? But then I reflected on how my spirit and Roy's had intermingled and grown in one another over the years we were together.

Throughout our marriage, we enjoyed hosting out-of-town guests in our home and cooking for friends. One summer Sunday morning, Roy and I were fixing brunch for an old friend, who sat on a barstool sipping her latte. Roy scraped the chopped red pepper and onion from the cutting board to the sauté pan while I whipped up the eggs and grated the cheese for a frittata. He brushed my ear as he reached past me for a spatula. I brought the bowl of eggs to the stove and bumped him with a gentle hip check before pouring them into the frying pan.

"Don't forget to put up the umbrella," I reminded him—we'd be eating on the deck.

He handed me his spatula and headed outside.

"Wow," our friend said, "it's like you two are dancing. I don't know many people who are synced like that."

This syncing of spirit was one outcome of love. Christ seemed to be asking this of his disciples in a far more spiritual and less human way than Roy and I had experienced.

"Apart from me," Christ said, "you can do nothing at all." He begged the disciples to continue living in his love, and to love one another. He seemed to say, I've given you everything I can. Now it's up to you.

Jesus continued his audacious claims to divine wisdom in the image of a vine giving life to its branches. His parable had some religious history. In the Old Testament, Israelites (God's chosen people) were often referred to as God's "choice vine." And this unfamiliar man, Jesus, with his strange power to teach and heal, suggested it all came from himself, as God, instead of from the God of their tradition. Bold stuff. The disciples probably had only a vague idea that Jesus was entrusting them with creating a new order on earth. And that he had precious little time to teach them about it. But in his entreaty, he asked them to comprehend the possibility of staying synced.

He knew their spirits would contract under the weight of grief. In his own grief about leaving them, he gave them a new vision, begged them to continue his work, and asked them to love one another. Then he sent them into a mind-boggling unknown.

I related to those twelve men when I sat on my mother's couch and repeated, "I just don't know what to do." The vision I'd created for my life, taken for granted, and lived with for thirty-three years suddenly evaporated. I couldn't seem to get people to understand the depth of my perplexity.

A friend said, "Maybe you're supposed to be doing exactly what you're doing."

Reading, crying, comforting myself, resting, taking time, and slowly building new connections. Creating a new vision for my life.

To embark on something as lofty as creating a new vision, I needed to step into something as basic as expanding my awareness beyond the pain. I wanted to draw on something larger than my constructed-self (the ego) to find a new way in the world, uncertain as it was sure to be. As I healed enough to move out of looping negative beliefs, thought processes, and emotional toxins, I cleared space in my mind, heart, and soul to connect with Divine Love in new ways. My true self felt safe enough to peek out from under the covers.

As an impressionable young spiritual seeker, I had learned that Jesus's parable of the vine and branches was about evangelism—about converting people to Christianity. Converts were evidence of fruit. Those who didn't produce fruit dried up to be cast into the fires of hell. Pretty scary stuff. But what if, instead, the parable was about co-creating with God in a more expansive way? What if it was about an invitation to connect with Divine Love, the true source of being? To discover an infinite source of creative expression?

Accessing my creative source and expressing myself was the work of my soul. It was my individual, constantly evolving expression of God in the world. Not perfect, but connected.

A different meaning in this passage about the vine and the branches emerged. "I am the vine and you are the branches" was not just connection, but an energetic synchronizing. The vine drew up nutrients from the earth and sent them out to branches that created fruit.

As a branch, I had shriveled and contracted. As I considered drawing new nutrients from a source of love, the possibility of moving on from healing and into growth enticed me just enough to take my first tiny steps.

Madeleine L'Engle says in *Walking on Water: Reflections on Faith and Art*, "God is constantly creating, in us, through us, with us, and to co-create with God is our human calling."

My opening was not nearly as transcendent. Roy died in an election year. Until then, I was caught up in the wave of optimism initiated by the publication of Barack Obama's *The Audacity of Hope* in 2006 and his election in 2008. My optimism was further fueled by anticipating a woman as president for the first time in our nation's history. When November 2016 rolled around and I started following the news again, my hopes were dashed by the election of President Donald Trump, the explosion of the Me Too movement, and the deadliest year of mass shootings in modern U.S. history. My personal despair seemed to be reflected back at me everywhere I looked.

How to stay connected and inspired?

If I was to create from a source other than my own ego, I wanted to find the same level of intimate connection with Love that the disciples experienced with Jesus. When I stepped into connection, what would I actually be connecting to? The Divine source I hoped to encounter had been described in many different ways by spiritual practitioners throughout history.

In another of his daily meditations, Richard Rohr compared it to striking a tuning fork and trying to resonate with true pitch, as with a musical instrument. "Once you are tuned," he wrote, "you will receive, and it has nothing to do with worthiness or the group you belong to, but only inner resonance, a capacity for mutuality which implies a basic humility."

Inner resonance. A capacity for mutuality. Basic humility.

Inner resonance piqued my interest. Connection to Love had something to do with a connection to the true self. There seemed to be something of transcendence in the experience of living from connection. I understood it to be deeply spiritual, but I couldn't seem to translate it into my daily life. I wanted to strip the fossilized clichés of my conservative past from the idea but also acknowledge its deep wisdom.

Rejecting the hierarchy that put educated men in charge of my spiritual experience seemed a good place to begin. I had been tiptoeing away for years, secretly, like leaving a crowded theater because I didn't like the movie. But I finally understood how the hierarchy limited my desire to co-create with God. My spirit was oppressed by a patriarchal interpretation of God that created a severely limited landscape of feminine experience. This oppression damaged my soul. Ironically, as a pastor's wife, I always felt like a stranger in church settings.

I once sat in an adult Sunday school class as three men dominated the discussion, even though the group was split fairly equally between men and women. The question presented was, "What are the signs of a healthy church?" The leader suggested financial stability and accountability as the signs to look for. Nods of agreement moved through the group. My discomfort and frustration simmered over a bit. I gave him a rather unkind, hard stare. The ocean of masculine authority that everyone else seemed to be swimming in with ease was drowning me.

"I think the health of a congregation is reflected in how the members treat one another," I offered.

The God of my forefathers, I was relieved to finally whisper, may not be the God for me. As my understanding of Divine Love expanded, I sought the balance of feminine spirituality. When it came to spiritual community, I was no longer willing to check my feminine spirit at the door, especially my sensibility and intuition. A creative understanding about how God danced in my world needed its place in my spiritual life.

Imagination played a new role in this exploration. The first Christmas after Roy died was an uncharted day of family togetherness, infused with a gaping hole where he should have been. None of us had any idea what to do, least of all me. But by the second Christmas, I had grown aware enough to see what my adult children were hoping for. In a million little ways, through questions about menus and worship options and ways to recognize their father, it began to dawn on me. They wanted me to be the family leader. Because half their leadership team was missing.

He had sat at the head of the table. He had led the holiday prayers. He had made most of the jokes. Even though I'd always led the holiday-related planning, they wanted me to participate in a new way. And so, with quivering uncertainty, I acknowledged my new role as the lone family leader.

The kids didn't want to be brought into every decision; they wanted me to make some decisions for them, to give the holiday structure and safe boundaries. During Advent, I spent a lot of time imagining what a good matriarchal leader would do in my situation. I didn't read about it or question others, I just imagined it.

Stories from my past reading served me well. I thought about the mother in *Little House on the Prairie*. I thought about Marmee in *Little Women*. I thought about the mother in *A Tree Grows in Brooklyn* who chose to throw away the leftover coffee from the pot each day as a single, defiant act of waste in a life of poverty. I thought of women I'd read about more recently in *The Nightingale* and *All the Light We Cannot See*, who inspired me with the strength and courage they brought to their loved ones during uncertainty and suffering. I found archetypes in the literary figures that inspired me to access the same in myself. I stepped into the holidays with a plan.

Sam and I spent Christmas Eve making lobster ravioli. I got to watch my adult son show off his skills as a chef—I was the novice in the kitchen for a change. He insisted he needed a ravioli form, so I drove to our town's treasure of a kitchen store on its busiest day of the year to find him one. We drank a little. We laughed a lot. Flour covered both of us and most of the kitchen counters. We wrapped up those little dumplings and stored them to eat the next day.

On Christmas morning, we all gingerly greeted one another when my daughter and her husband arrived, having picked up my mom on their way. We gathered in the family room and opened gifts with measured steps toward gratitude and joy.

Then I gave them their last gifts, with a gentle explanation about acknowledging and including dad. I asked them to open the gifts at the same time. Tears flowed as they turned the pages of the book I'd created for each of them: collected images from the slideshow at Roy's celebration of life ceremony. A keepsake of some of the best moments of our lives together.

We took our time. We laughed through tears and acknowledged that it was fine and good to do so. Then we hugged and comforted each other, dried our tears, set the books beneath the tree with the other gifts, and stumbled our way through another holiday dinner.

Imagining, an important tool of spiritual development, had been absent in my religious education. Why was I never taught about the creative potential in my imaginal life? One likely reason was the endemic oppression of creativity in our educational system. My childhood schooling focused on rote memorization and knowledge performance. Especially into high school, classes in music, arts and crafts, and other forms of creativity were considered "easy A" courses that students took only to bolster their grade point average.

In contrast, recent research demonstrated the important role of creativity as a foundation of invention. In a 2013 study published in *Economic Development Quarterly*, a team of multidisciplinary researchers studied a group of honors college graduates. They found that those who owned businesses or patents had received up to eight times more exposure to the arts as children than the general public. Researchers also found that 93 percent of the graduates reported musical training at some point in their lives, compared to only 34 percent of average adults, as reported by the National Endowment for the Arts. The graduates also reported higher than average involvement in visual arts, acting, dance, and creative writing.

This same creativity, this same cultivation of imagination, is also necessary for spiritual healing and growth. In *The Healing Imagination,* Ann Ulanov suggests that "rescue and healing demand the imagination. It brings food to the exhausted soul." If we encouraged equal attention to imaginative creativity in psychological and spiritual development, could it not also influence our ability to creatively imagine our healing? Our lives?

As I met with and read the works of other people breaking through imposed limitations to engage their imagination, I also explored Richard Rohr's second characteristic of the tuning fork image: mutuality. I found teachers and writers who were already cultivating their connection to true frequency. I enjoyed tea and conversation with a woman who described her challenge in defining her cosmology—her belief system about the origin and general structure of the universe. I was brought up short. I thought, you mean you can do that?

Entering into my imaginal space took me far afield from the masculine, intellectual expressions, hierarchies, power structures, laws, and judgment I'd experienced in institutional religion. Embodied spirituality, a practice of the heart, carried me into feminine experiences of connection, unfolding, and emergence. I experienced forgiveness, compassion, grace, and mercy. I embraced a new freedom to act on the wisdom from my own creative connections and experiences. The freedom to co-create.

Intrinsic to co-creation was the third aspect of Rohr's description: humility. Searching for coherence in my daily practice, I encountered many opportunities to unite the dark and light aspects of my self.

Listening had always been difficult for me. I anticipated what people were going to say before the last three or five words came out of their mouth. And I, like many people, had a quick response. Same with trying to listen to God. I anticipated what God was going to say and was ready with a reply. But the peace of silence kept courting me, and I found myself more and more drawn to it. Mostly in meditation, but also in conversation, I tried to be in a state of quiet reception, in the feminine place of listening rather than positing. In the depths of silence, I befriended stillness. Then nothingness.

And in nothingness, connection appeared. A little trickle of nourishment flowed into the withered vine. I shifted from thoughts and ideas to experience, as a felt sense. I was open-hearted. Humility breathed into my very humanness. I saw anger and rage needing a container as well as an expression. I saw deep sadness and grief hiding behind resentments. I saw myself as a victim waiting by the pool for someone to rescue me; I saw a self-righteous superiority blocking me from connection. I saw weakness and frailty, strength and courage. I saw my mortality.

Coming upon these hard realities, I practiced softening into self-forgiveness by reminding myself it was okay. I chuckled at my illusions. I got to know my heart a bit better. I became aware of the physical sensations of emotional pain: the clutching in the chest, the stinging in the nose and eyes. I became familiar with the rising sensation in my solar plexus that I came to know as anger, and of the moments when I let down the protective blinds over my heart. And I might just have caught a glimpse of my shy soul—just a flash of a glimpse, really, but sometimes I felt its shining energy. The elusive glimmers of connection. Embodied and inward.

As I connected to my soul, I gained more confidence in expressing my unique spiritual journey rather than following an external guide. In *Walking on Water*, Madeleine L'Engle said it this way: "If our lives are truly 'hid with Christ in God,' the astounding thing is that this hiddenness is revealed in all that we do and say and write."

And then one day I said to my therapist, "You know, I'm getting kind of tired of just reading what other people think and feel. I want to know what I think and feel. But I can't seem to slow myself down enough to write it down. My thoughts move too fast to get them into the pen and onto the paper. How can I slow myself down to listen?"

"Maybe you don't need to slow down in order to write," he suggested. "Maybe you need to write in order to slow it all down."

A coherence grew from that epiphany. I had separated my meditative experience from everything else. He encouraged me to bring it into everything. To open to exploration. To find curiosity. To allow every creative expression to grow from a series of day-to-day building blocks coming together into something new.

Some days I got close. Other days I couldn't even see the possibility in the distance. It felt impossible to engage with vision in the depths of suffering, to maintain hope in the face of despair, to connect when I felt betrayed and abandoned. And yet, by grace, my shriveling little branch found water and nurturance, the tuning fork sounding in me a newly inspired vision. A returning desire to, like the daffodils in spring, poke my head out into the world and sync up again with the flow and rhythm of time.

THE OTHER SIDE

My daughter, in her thirties, had a job that required travel. One evening, we talked about an upcoming trip and she teasingly asked if I thought she should pack everything in Ziploc bags. That's how I used to pack their clothes for vacations: one outfit in each gallon-sized Ziploc bag. Each day of vacation, they picked an outfit. At the end of the day, they returned the dirty clothes to the bag. In my defense, this OCD habit came from decades of business travel. In my twenties and thirties, I worked in the events industry and I, too, traveled a lot. As most frequent travelers do, I had a system for my trips. I bragged that I could be packed to go anywhere in thirty minutes.

A year after Roy died, I was invited to a twenty-fifth anniversary celebration for a program I had worked on during those traveling years. I hadn't yet taken a trip, and I was nervous about it. But it was like riding a bike. It was almost a comfort to go through the old travel rituals. I carefully selected my wardrobe, packed my bag, shuttled to the airport, stood in taxi lines, checked into the hotel, dressed for the social event.

I felt the professional me return as I stepped from my hotel room wearing high heels and a knee-length black silk jacket I'd discovered in a back corner of my closet. I reunited with old business associates and polished up my rusty networking skills. I dabbled with the idea of working again. I initiated conversations, probing for opportunities. I returned home and made a few tentative follow-up calls. Nothing transpired.

Nothing.

My attempts to return to the old, established connections and patterns were no longer an option. My healing, at its core, required change. And I didn't like it. I've known women who leapt into change in their lives with shocking spontaneity and grace. I, however, liked my changes in small, barely perceptible increments—so one day I could wake up and say, oh! I've changed! How delightful!

Gradual as I wanted it to be, the change required after Roy's death felt cataclysmic. Oh, the lovely security of the familiar, the routine, the expected, even the dark rooms of well-padded despair I'd designed for myself. And yet ... how could there be thriving in the stagnant complacence of the known, regardless of how safe and secure it was?

Roy's death catapulted me into the unknown. I felt like Sandra Bullock in the movie *Gravity*—especially in the scene where she floated, untethered, in space. Her connection to the mothership severed, she had no certainty that she wouldn't float off into the universe forever. What a great metaphor. I recalled that scene frequently.

Jesus's followers discovered the same truth when they, too, tried to return to the familiar. After Jesus's death, they experienced what must have felt like a cataclysmic change, as I had. They lost not only a loved one but a teacher and guide who had opened up a world of mysterious events and connections. This leader sparked their hearts with the possibility of a new order on earth and a new understanding of heaven. He loved them and built in them a new vision for their lives.

But then he was crucified. According to Judaic law, he could not be buried the same day, as it was the sabbath. So his loved ones took him down from the cross, set his body in a small cave, and covered the opening with a large stone. The following morning when they returned, his body was gone. Christian believers ascribe the miracle of his resurrection to that story. Afterward, again confirming the theory of resurrection, the story told us that Jesus appeared to his loved ones, apparently in full bodily form, at random moments.

In the disorienting space of early grief, not quite knowing what to do next, it appeared that the disciples had lost sight of Jesus's promises and directions. Especially the disciple Peter, who had passionately pinned his very being, his identity, his self, on those promises. Peter had taken the leap to unbridled trust.

As tension with religious leaders grew, some followers saw trouble brewing and dropped away. Jesus asked his remaining inner circle of twelve if they wanted to go away also. Peter's response was so full of trust. "Lord, to whom shall we go?" he asked. "You have words of eternal life. And we have believed and have come to know that you are the holy one of God."

But shortly after Christ's death, it appeared his inner circle had lost sight of their vision. They did not leave Jesus; he left them. What were they to do?

Only Peter had not lost his trust. I imagined him in his confused grief saying, I guess I'll go fishing. And the others saying, Okay, yeah, what else are we going to do. We'll go with you.

Like the disciples, I really didn't know what else to do. My longing to return to the way things were took up much of my early healing space. Because I had worked in Roy's business, after he died I didn't have a job to return to. I found myself in grief-group meetings, envious of anyone who had a job, career, vocation, something to go back to. Some piece of "self" they could pick up again and not have to re-create. I suspected that I didn't yet have the fortitude to work. But I wanted it. I wanted something from the "old way." Some sure piece of me.

For me, and for the disciples, the old way was unproductive. Peter and the guys went out and fished all night and caught nothing.

Nothing.

It was tough to sit in a void. The old things made me feel some sense of sure-footedness on ground slipping away like scree on a precipice. Since I didn't know what else to do, I tried returning to what I'd done before. However, my healing required something different. It wasn't yet about doing.

Well, then, what was it about? I wondered.

It was about inward transformation. And inward transformation required just being and receiving. Somehow, in ways I couldn't yet understand, it involved letting go and surrendering to a mystery.

As dawn rose on the disciples' futile night with their fishing nets, they encountered a stranger on the beach. The stranger suggested they try again, this time casting their nets on the opposite side of the boat. They set out under these instructions—a slight adjustment to what they'd been doing—and, the story says, had trouble hauling in the nets weighed down by their extraordinary catch.

As in the disciples' experience, my healing began with a simple idea: maybe just try the other side of the boat. I didn't make sweeping changes in the wake of my grief, and this story supported my decision. Well-meaning friends, suggestions in grief books, and the words in my grief group all told me not to make any big decisions in the first year. They didn't have to worry about me. I didn't plan to.

I wasn't inclined to make grand gestures. My journey through grief didn't include a new career, a soul trek to India, or a new house or city. But the tumultuous change of losing Roy was only a precursor to the infinite subtle and minute changes I encountered over the next few years. Like the disciples, all I could do was launch the same boat I'd been using and maybe just try the net on the other side.

I didn't want to go to the grocery store by myself, handle the health insurance, take out the trash, mow the lawn, find new friends, plan different vacations, search for a job, have the furnace replaced, work with the roofers. I wanted to take my net like I always had and cast it into the sea. I willed the fish to jump in like they had in my life with Roy. I didn't want to accept that in a single moment, everything in my life changed. But I slowly accepted a new reality by taking my net and casting it in a different way, to a place I'd never thrown it. By learning a new way of receiving.

In this opening, the grand gesture was not in the activity, but in the boundless trust required.

In the story of the disciples and the nets, during those early morning hours after they'd recast their nets and hauled in the amazing catch, one of the disciples told Peter it was Jesus who had spoken to them. He pointed to Jesus standing on the shore. When Peter realized who it was (and here's the trust, embedded in his spirit) he threw himself into the sea to get to Jesus. He swam to the shore and saw the bounty of fish in the nets, his friends laughing and struggling to land the catch, and there was Jesus, as if he were saying, I knew you'd get here. See, I laid the fire and already started grilling fish.

Roy, at times, had a knack for anticipating something I might enjoy, and he loved watching me come upon the surprise. A challenging ski run. A delightful fishing stream. A new glass of sauvignon blanc at a local hangout. He had this way of looking at me and raising one eyebrow, a playful sort of "yeah, I saw this coming and knew you'd like it." That was love. That was my experience of feeling seen and being known. That's what Jesus did as the disciples approached the shore.

Could I trust God to know and love me in this way too? Could I leap with Peter's abandon into a love far deeper and wider than the love I'd experienced with Roy? Could I trust that it would come, now, from other places than my marriage? And what would my own reckless abandonment to this trust look like? How would this change where I put my time and energy? Could I again find a passion in my life equal to the complex love I knew with Roy? How did it work for Peter?

If I could see more into Peter's relationship with Jesus, I could also see what Peter lost when Christ died. Or what he thought he lost. What kind of trust did it take for him to get beyond the grief and disappointment of this loss to become a leader in this radical new movement? What did it take for him to move beyond despair—perhaps even cynicism, anger, resentment, and shock—into transformational trust?

Partly, it was about testing. In another version of the story of Jesus walking on water, the disciples thought it was a ghost walking toward them. Jesus told them not to be afraid. Peter replied, "If it's really you, command me to come to you on the water." When Jesus told him to come, Peter got out of the boat and walked toward him on the water.

Madeleine L'Engle wrote of this experience, "When Jesus called Peter to come to him across the water, Peter, for one brief, glorious moment, remembered how and strode with ease across the lake. This is how we are meant to be, and then we forget, and we sink. But if we cry out for help (as Peter did) we will be pulled out of the water; we won't drown. And if we listen, we will hear; and if we look, we will see."

During my transition, the object of my trust was sorely challenged. This trust asked for a relinquishing of all I had created and come to depend on for my entire life. It asked me to trust in something beyond my constructed-self. It required faith in the healing experiences, but it also threatened to reopen wounds. I tried. Slowly. But would I throw myself out of the boat? No way.

Skeptical as I felt, I tentatively opened into a place of receivership. All I'd relinquished would not be conveniently replaced. What filled the newly emptied space had to be tenaciously created, but also humbly received. It was a vulnerable choice, but not a passive one. Paradoxically, it was undergirded by both action and surrender.

Before Roy died, my idea of the grief experience was taking time to rest only to wake up one day and resume life as I had known it. A light dawned as I pieced together the truth: if I was going to move out of darkness and pain, I was going to have to change how I lived my life. Every day would require doing something new or different. Before Roy died, I had the luxury of waking up most days to a cup of steaming tea, fixed just how I liked it with cream and honey, delivered by an indulgent husband to my nightstand.

On those mornings, I enjoyed a slow waking as I sipped, easing into my day. From our bed I could see into the sink area of our bathroom. I loved watching Roy shave after his shower—a purely masculine routine he took for granted, exercised in the intimacy of our life together. The way he unconsciously leaned into the sink as the razor moved up from the base of his neck over his chin. The care he took where the corners of his mustache met his lips. Thus, my earliest change required me to get out of bed and make my own tea. It was many months before I removed his shaving things from below his sink in the bathroom. It didn't sound like much. But it was.

Change was an inconvenient, humbling, ill-defined, and desperate business.

After all my visits to doctors and my attempts to medicate the anxiety and depression, I finally surrendered to the process. And then I could receive. As I surrendered into weakness, my kids brought me enormous strength. As I surrendered into incompetence, my friends brought helping hands and tender empathy. As I surrendered into floating adrift on an ocean of idleness, old acquaintances offered meaningful work.

On some days, instead of lying in bed until I had to get up to meet someone or go somewhere, I chose to wake up and thank God for breathing. I could receive breath. I still think that's a pretty good way to start my day.

I hung a plaque reminding me to "start each day with a grateful heart" where I could see it from my bed. When I first woke, I tried to feel a ray of gratitude through the heavy fog of grief, like finding the tiny grains of sugar sprinkled in a bowl of oatmeal. Lots and lots of blandness and sameness, and then a hint of something sweet. I kept eating to see if I'd get another taste.

I found a grief group. A little receiving. A sprinkle of sugar. I made new widow friends. More receiving. Another taste of sweetness. I woke up another morning and cast my net on the other side, yet again struggling with my fear of an uncertain future.

Change.

A give and take of trust and vulnerability, intention and surrender, were the stuff of healing. In an intimate dance with the Divine, each person, each situation, each experience, created a unique series of steps and rhythms for rebuilding my life.

And then my steps became less tentative. One day on the Camino, I was struck with clarity about what I had to do—what each piece of my life had led me to, including Roy's death. Just outside the village of Foncebadón, I came upon a small iron cross atop a pole that was at least sixty feet tall. It was planted in a mound of stones, and people were scrambling up for photos. The cross was part of a ritual I'd read about in my guidebook. As my journey on the Camino commenced, I was encouraged to pick up a stone to carry in my pack as a token of love or blessing. When I arrived at the cross, about halfway through, I could lay it down as a symbol of the collective journey.

That warm and sunny day, I took the stone from my pack and tossed it on the pile. Beyond the cross was a small park with picnic tables and benches. I sat down and pulled out my journal, making a long list of all the things keeping me from pursuing the creative life I'd always longed for. When I arrived home, I stopped taking random classes, quit the tennis team, built my social connections with more intention, and sat down in front of my computer every day to write.

In the end, suffering brought me great clarity. It wasn't a utopia—all of life's challenges continued presenting themselves to me. I still cared for my aging mother, still supported my children as they found their way in the world, still worked to accept solitude as a way of life. But I knew what inspired me to jump out of the boat with reckless abandon: I decided to trust in a writing life. I didn't want to waste my time on anything else.

Casting my net on the right-hand side.

THE SHEEP

ONE THING I KNOW I CAN COUNT ON is that March will come again this year. As it does every year. This year on March 8, I'll take out the birthday book I made for my son and relive the day he came into my life. This year on March 16, I'll take out the birthday book my mother made for me and relive significant events of my own life. This year on March 18, I'll take out the memory book of images from Roy's celebration of life service and relive our time together.

In Liane Moriarty's delightfully sharp and witty book *Nine Perfect Strangers*, she offers us a character, Zoe, a young woman who lost her twin brother to suicide three years before the story took place.

In one scene, Zoey's boyfriend asks, "So are you going to have to spend the week in January with your parents for the rest of your whole life?"

"Uh, yeah," she says.

Before Roy died, I, like most people who haven't lost a significant person, knew I would be over it after a year. But as the clocked ticked down to the first anniversary of his death, I panicked because I'd barely gotten over the initial shock in a year, let alone the loss. As I came upon the two-year anniversary, I was fully functioning. I appeared to have gotten over it. But I hadn't. Year three rolled around and I realized my truth: I will not be getting over this.

I've moved my wedding ring from my left hand to a necklace I wear near my heart. While my marriage is no longer a reality in the physical world, our heart relationship is eternal. Will I, in fact, mark the anniversary of Roy's death every year for the rest of my life? Uh, yeah. In the same way I'll carry my love for Roy in my heart for the rest of my life. In the same way I believe my husband carried his love for me into another realm, where it expanded and returned to me in memories and images and dreams. Because our love hasn't died. It's immortal.

I could never have wrapped my arms around that idea unless I'd experienced it with Roy. Only then could I see it in Jesus's message to his disciples, especially his beloved Peter.

In the same story where Jesus appeared to them while they were fishing, he had a compelling conversation with Peter. Jesus asked three times whether Peter loved him more than the other disciples did. Each time, Peter confirmed his love, even exclaiming after the third time, "Jesus, you know everything. You must know how much I love you."

Each time, Jesus replied, "Feed my sheep."

Feed my sheep. Was Peter as challenged to understand Jesus's meaning as I was? Jesus pushed Peter to exasperation. Only he knew of Peter's future role as a leader of their new community. Only he foresaw the price Peter would pay, sacrificed as a martyr. Maybe he wanted to remind Peter—to almost force him—to store within his heart those feelings of love for Christ that he could carry into the unknown. Because his love would be immortal.

To explore the truth hidden in this comment, I had to unravel yet another set of limiting beliefs I received in my childhood. I was taught that "feeding Jesus's sheep" meant teaching new believers the messages of the Bible: to do as you're told and teach other people what you learn. A closed-loop belief system.

Here was another unraveling opportunity. What if, in a more universal sense, the sheep reference was to the human soul? The innocent, gentle, tender, interior part of Peter, and Jesus's other friends, and me? The part of all of us seeking to be loved, vulnerable to the wolves, longing for nurture and protection, thriving in creative expression and community participation. What if Jesus was trying to invite us all to tend to our soul, and the souls of others, so we could engage in life with purpose and meaning?

The phrase "feed my sheep" invited me to look more deeply into what my soul required for well-being. I paid more attention to the ways in which the spiritual nurturing I desired was an intermingling of my longings for consolation and acceptance. But, as I'd heard it said, "there is no there there." What I sought externally could only be found within. As spiritual healing grew in me, I came more in touch with what wanted to be expressed through me. This expression, both infinite and particular, was what Christ referred to when he implored Peter to feed his sheep.

Participating in life from an interior place—what I learned to call feeding my soul—arose out of felt experience rather than intellectual understanding. Each new generation of theologians has made an exerted effort at cognitive knowledge, which has provided us with centuries of robust beliefs but fallen short in the expression of love, joy, and peace. Because those were felt experiences. Instead of intellectual debate, Jesus encouraged Peter to share his experience of his relationship with Christ. What did you see, hear, feel?

In this New Testament story, a group of outcasts, lost and despairing, were engaged in what would today be called a social experiment: to live out Jesus's vision for a radical new order based on love. Being with Jesus changed them so much that they had a passion to share those changes, along with their stories of living in community, their poetic expressions of love (love is patient, love is kind, love is never jealous or envious or boastful or rude), and the creative workings of justice, mercy, and forgiveness.

A transformational experience also changed me. I listened more to my gut reaction and conversed more with my higher self. I tried to take life less seriously as I learned to dance with the angels of mirth. When it looked like I could possibly make a mistake or fail at any endeavor, I tried to bring more lightheartedness to my inner and outer work. Lightheartedness became creative fuel for me. When I could let go of my anxiety about performing for a remote, capricious, and punishing deity, I could explore feeling loved, comforted, protected, and safe.

Suffering softened my edges. In that softening, I gained access to gentler emotions and responses like patience, acceptance, delight, and humor. I spent less energy fending off anticipated tragedies and more energy finding beauty and comfort in the present moment. I laughed more and wept more.

I shed old patterns of criticism, expectation, entitlement. I no longer had the odd luxury of saying, "Thank God that didn't happen to me." It did happen to me. And it could happen to me again. I didn't have the false protection of an "us vs. them" polarity when it came to human suffering. I was finding my way to compassion by receiving the compassion of others.

As dawn slowly peeked over the horizon each day, I looked beyond my own experience. I learned there was a term for this: expansiveness. My suffering was a microcosm of universal suffering in the world. I could listen without turning away as friends and sometimes strangers needed to share their suffering. Rather than change the subject or avoid feeling powerless in the face of death, illness, abuse, confusion, or anger, I acknowledged how powerless I was to change their circumstance. But I could pause to be present with them. I no longer had to fix it. Nor did I have to shield myself from it. I simply listened and let the emotion of their experience flow.

My own emotional soap opera became less interesting. Allowing my emotions to stay present, I took time for them, nurtured my spirit, and showed up in relationships with less need for someone else to take care of me. I relieved myself of the burden of taking on the emotions of others. Relationships took on new meaning as I allowed more space for others to be themselves rather than someone who was required to make me feel safe.

Finally, I fanned the flames of lightheartedness that had begun to rekindle. In our marriage vows, Roy promised to always make me laugh. Laughter and joy are the hallmarks of new relationships, of course, but we committed to sustaining it. His sense of humor could be the stuff of corny jokes and silly gestures—he liked to perform for the vacation Bible school crew each summer. My kids still talk about one time during the safari-themed program, when he came onstage wearing a pith helmet with a donut taped to the top, pretending to search for the lost confection. He had a sanctuary full of kids yelling to him and pointing to his hat as he paced the stage.

More often, though, what set my heart alight were the unexpected and surprising gestures. Early in our marriage, I took a weekend-long self-defense course that ended with an informal ceremony for family and friends.

"Wear something cool," I said to him as I left the house, wanting him to be comfortable in the overheated gym.

He showed up in a tuxedo and winked at me from the audience.

"I didn't mean James Bond cool," I said when he hugged me later.

"I knew what you meant," he whispered in my ear.

Now, more often, it's my son or daughter who tickles my funny bone with their keen eye for the absurd. And it's okay that they're frequently laughing at me. As I've given up my tightly controlled sense of organization, I find myself losing things more and more. My phone and my glasses, mostly, but hats, gloves, the random set of keys.

One day, my daughter came over as I was making dinner. I'd just finished draining the pasta water into the sink and was moving on to something else when she rushed over to the stove. "Oh my God, mother," she said as she turned off the burner, still red-hot, with a flick of her wrist. "Don't make me have to put you in a home."

She was kidding, right?

Spiritual healing reoriented my worldview and challenged the symbols of my interior life. I understood mythology in a new way. Myths, as collections of stories and ideas, may not be literally true, but I came to see how they illuminated deeper spiritual truths. Feeding my soul meant consciously drawing on stories to experience truth in infinite ways through my imagination. I found essential nourishment in poetry, mythology, symbolism, and art. I grew more curious about the stories that defined me, whether familial or cultural. I appreciated feeling connected to my history, part of a tribe—even a tribe filled with paradox and conundrum. But I also felt driven to expand my tribal story out from the symbols of Christianity to those of other cultures.

Tribes have long used storytelling to honor and share their collective beliefs. I always cherished the Bible stories of my tradition. When Roy and I did children's ministry together, our favorite program was "Children and Worship." It called on the best principles of faith development to help young children build an internal connection to the mythology of our tribe: Christianity. Members of our congregation contributed skills like woodworking, painting, and organizing to create a collection of storytelling boxes. For the box about Noah, they made a beautifully crafted, to-scale copy of the ark, complete with pairs of elephants, giraffes, and horses. While adults worshipped in the sanctuary, children spent time in the smaller chapel, gathered in a circle on the floor. Alone or in small groups, children could select a box and use the manipulatives—from carved boats to fishing nets to mustard seeds—to retell and re-create biblical stories in their own words. It was the ritual of childhood storytelling at its best.

How could I, in a similar way, use the mythology of my roots as a foundation to build one more suited to my soul? It was no small question in our global, multimedia culture, but in the same way, it could be easier than ever with Google and technology-driven library systems. I found expansion exceedingly important, as it figured heavily in my ongoing healing. I connected with the Hindu goddess Kali, who showed me a fierce and protective feminine archetype; the Chinese goddess Quan Yin, for compassion; and Mary Magdalene for a lovely, and unfortunately unrecognized, balance of feminine divinity and Christ's passion.

If my mythology was worth anything, it had to serve me daily. My daily drive. My daily meals. My daily conversations. My daily conflicts. But it also had to expand far beyond my limited experience to also embrace a diverse global tribe. This made Jesus's command to "feed my sheep" just as radical today as it was when he said it. What would society look like if we operated from a place of connected experience? How could spiritual healing transform our collective interiority and reshape our exterior world without deteriorating into cliché? I saw the infinite implications of the question. Like the disciples, I found myself on the shores of exploring it in my ongoing process of spiritual healing.

"Feeding my sheep" no longer meant telling people about Christ and caring for new followers. To continue breathing life into this teaching, I created my own interpretation: furthering loving consciousness in its expression here and now. Recognizing the creative possibility in everything we do together, and living from that space. Only my limited beliefs kept me from living in a place of beauty, believing in truth, and encouraging the expression of the human spirit.

Admittedly, as spiritual healing opened me to live from my soul, the shifts in consciousness I experienced weren't exactly the stuff of a new world order. They were small building blocks. But aren't these the building blocks on which all relationships are built? And aren't relationships—with self, work, creative expression, and other people—the building blocks on which communities are built? Jesus's reference to shepherding was about healing the soul; any expression and giving of loving consciousness qualified.

In Madeleine L'Engle's words from *Walking on Water*, "The discipline of creation is an effort toward wholeness."

As I write this, it's been four years since Roy's death, and I now split my time between my own home and my eighty-seven-year-old mother's house. She can no longer drive, so I manage her medical care and errands and generally keep an eye on her. We recently went to a weekly iron infusion at the hospital only to find that the clinic had been moved to a different location in the building. I pushed her wheelchair through the halls, following the taped-up signs to the new room, which was lined with recliners and makeshift dividers. Through a wall of windows I could see the light snowfall, typical spring weather in Colorado.

A nurse helped me get my mom situated in the heated recliner. As she gently tapped the inside of my mother's arm, searching for a good vein, she said casually, "They did a pretty good job converting this old ER waiting room, didn't they?"

I braced as if expecting impact. I looked around—there was the entrance I'd walked through on that horrible day, now closed off to public traffic. There was the reception counter where I'd checked in, numb and dazed. I realized that we were sitting in the exact location of the prefab room where I'd received the news.

The nurse chatted with my mother as I took slow, deep breaths, concentrating on my feet grounded on the floor, asking my body not to tremble. I had fifteen minutes while the iron serum dripped from the bag into my mother's vein to process the memory of those hours. Again. To let emotion rise and flood my system and move through. But now, I discovered, I could sit in the same room and remember the details. It would be okay, I realized. I could do this. I closed my eyes for a while and felt myself falling into the arms of my therapist. It was an imprint I'd received into my spirit—it would always be there when I needed to surrender into the arms of Love.

My need for spiritual healing had been but a grain of sand in a world longing for healing and connection. Perhaps I was opening to yet another truth: that even the greatest human discoveries at this point in evolution were still preschool-level revelations in the vast creative potential of loving consciousness. At best, we played at understanding.

I took it all very seriously. Like my preschoolers. Like one little girl who tried so very hard to zip up her coat with creative ways to make it work, her entire little body tensing up until she screamed, pulled it off, and threw it on the floor. Watching her, I thought, That's how humans are as we try to figure out our lives in relation to loving consciousness.

It's been said that we can't heal from the same place within us that experienced the wound. Healing requires expanding our own consciousness, connecting with a higher self in our soul, and opening to Divine Consciousness, sometimes called the indwelling of the Holy Spirit.

Like my preschoolers, I got frustrated by my failings and shortcomings as I practiced living from my soul. At times, I still wanted to throw it aside and live from a less conscious place. I told myself it would be easier. Maybe it would. But spiritual healing continued to invite me into the possibilities of a richer, more authentic life. As I struggled to understand this, Jesus's instruction to "feed my sheep" reminded me to nurture my soul every day. It invited me into the sheepfold. Where I could be well.

ACKNOWLEDGMENTS

I WANT TO BEGIN BY THANKING my grief-group friend Martha Fosdick, who encouraged me early on to get back to writing. Thank you for reading my ugly first draft and cheering me on.

Thank you to our family therapist, Sam Latona, who has done so much for our family, always gently and patiently pointing me back to my Divine Healer.

Thank you to Kristie Steinbock, my traditional Chinese medicine doctor, who steps into the ring and uses her gifts to heal others every day.

Thank you to my writing partner, Joan Heiman, who walked with me from the first clumsy draft through the final edits. Her experience, wisdom, and camaraderie kept me going.

Thank you to my beta readers for your insightful comments and corrections: Julie Burgess, Kendra Johnson, Nancy Kepner, Kathy Padilla and JoAnn Zeman.

Thank you to my editor, Molly McCowan at Inkbot Editing, for her wisdom as we shaped my jumble of words into a story.

And special thanks to everyone who offered their kindness, compassion, encouragement, and light as I stumbled along. You know who you are.

Each person brought their small contribution, we blessed it, and miracles happened.

PERMISSIONS